Ministry with Young Adults: The Search for Intimacy

faithQuest
the trade imprint of Brethren Press
Elgin, Illinois

Ministry With Young Adults:
The Search for Intimacy

Cover design by Jeane Healy

Library of Congress Cataloging-in-Publication Data
Ministry with young adults—Search for intimacy
    /Julie Garber, editor.
        p. ca.
    ISBN 0-87178-773-3
    1. Church work with young adults.
    I. Garber, Julie
    BV4445.S43 1991
    259'.084'2—dc20   91-31651
                                                            CIP

Manufactured in the United States of America

Ministry With Young Adults:
The Search for Intimacy

Ministry with Young Adults: The Search for Intimacy

Introduction

A primary task of young adults, said developmental theorist Eric Erikson, is to move toward intimacy rather than isolation. His theory of human development assumed that the focus of adolescence is the search for identity and individuation. When a person moves into young adulthood, the focus shifts to intimacy. As a person leaves his or her parent's home, establishing and strengthening relationships becomes a high priority. A young adult is seeking a new network of support: close friendships and perhaps a "significant other." It may be a time of getting married and having children. Young adults are also re-configuring their relationships with their parents, from that of a child to that of an adult. In all of these developments, there is a deep concern about relationships and a search for intimacy.

Many observers of our culture believe that young adults today are among the most spiritually-oriented people, carefully striving to find a meaningful relationship with God (which is another aspect of the search for intimacy). These observers also note that the spiritual hunger does not necessarily involve institutions such as the church. Many young adults even find that institutions impede their quest rather than aid it.

The climate for ministry with young adults in the '90s is very good given their high interest in spirituality—if our institutional failures do not get in the way. As young adults seek God, how can the church reach out to them in helpful ways?

I am frequently asked questions like, "Why don't young adults attend our church?" or "What are young adults looking for?" or "How can our church do a better job of reaching out to young adults?" These are important questions because young adults have much to contribute to the life of the church. This book will respond to those questions in very concrete and specific ways.

This book is designed to help congregations strengthen their ministries with this important age group. Why is young adult ministry important? Let me suggest three reasons:

1. Because of their sheer numbers. One third of the adult population is made up of young adults.

2. Because young adults have qualities that the church needs: creativity, energy, and enthusiasm.

3. Because the church is a valuable resource and support community for young adults who are asking questions about the meaning of life and searching for a faith they can believe.

Our ministry with young adults is an important one. Tex Sample, professor of church and society at St. Paul School of Theology in Minnesota, has said that the main reason why mainline churches have been declining in membership is that they have lost the participation of young adults.

In this book you will be challenged to find new ways of opening the doors of your church to include young adults who are searching for meaning and for belonging.

Chris Michael
Staff for Youth/Young Adult Ministry
Church of the Brethren

Intimacy and Community

Kim Yaussy Albright

While all three synoptic gospels relate the story of "a man" who asks Jesus what good deed he must do to inherit eternal life, only Matthew calls him a *young* man (Matt. 19:16ff). He is a young adult, and a rich young adult at that. We don't know how he became rich. Perhaps he inherited his family's fortune. Perhaps he earned his M.B.A. at the local university. At any rate, Matthew portrays the man as young.

Jesus says that this young man—in the prime of his life, just when things are going well—must sell what he possesses, give the money to the poor, and follow Jesus. If this is what must be done to enter into eternal life, the rich young man is not sure that living forever is worth the price. He leaves sorrowful, for he has many possessions.

We have to give the young man credit, I suppose, for even taking the risk of asking Jesus such an important question. He had followed all the commandments his whole life; he had done what he had been told to do; he had followed the letter of the law. But something was missing. He sensed his faith was lacking.

Jesus says to the young man, "If you wish to be *perfect*, go, sell . . . give . . . and come, follow me" (emphasis mine). The Greek word rendered as "perfect" in English might also be translated as "whole," "undivided," or "complete." To be perfect, then, is to be undivided in one's relationship with God, self, and others. In order to become whole, or undivided, one must detach oneself from anything that comes between the person and God. The separating factor for the rich young man is his wealth and possessions; these keep him from a complete relationship with God, himself, and others.

The biblical story of the rich young man bears significance for young adults today. Like the young man in the gospel story, young adults search for wholeness and intimacy—an "undividedness" in relationships with self, others, and God.

According to the psychologist Eric Erikson, the primary task of young adulthood is to establish intimacy and avoid isolation. Young adults also struggle to discover and assert their own identities. Many young adults thus experience tension between a yearning for *individuation*—being distinct, exercising one's own action—and a yearning for *connection*, *belonging*, and *intimacy*.

Sharon Parks, in her book *The Critical Years: The Young Adult Search for a Faith to Live By*, describes the central strength of the young adult as "the capacity to respond to visions of the world as it might become." Yet, young adults are also vulnerable. They are vulnerable to arrogance (thinking they know it all), estrangement (from themselves, friends, family, society), despair and meaninglessness ("What's the point? We're all going to die in a nuclear holocaust anyway"), and exploitation by mentors and communities (being "taken in" by cults).

What does all of this mean for the church? The church must respond to the needs and questions of young adults. The church must provide a *community* in which young adults can feel safe,

supported, encouraged, and even challenged in
their search for identity and intimacy.

But "community" means many things to many
people. I would like to define community as a
gathering of people connected with each other, yet
also differentiated from each other. In other
words, a community is where each one belongs,
yet each can be an individual. Furthermore, a
church community is that place where people are
challenged to think, change, and grow in their
faith ("sell all they have"), yet also a place where
people are included, forgiven, and accepted as
they are.

The church, then, must *create* a community in
which young adults may find the intimacy, meaning, and wholeness for which they search, in a
safe, yet challenging environment. The church can
do this by providing young adults with at least
three things: a meaningful ideology—a "dream" of
self, world, and God that resonates with the
young adult's life experience; a grounding community—a place in which and people with whom the
young adult can belong; and charismatic leadership—mentors who will awaken and call out the
potential of young adults.

First, the church can provide young adults with
a meaningful ideology. Young adults want to explore their Christian faith more deeply, whether it
is a faith they inherited or a newly adopted faith.
They want to dig down below the surface. They
want to "talk straight," ask hard questions, and
explore possible answers. The church can provide
an arena for exploring difficult and important
moral, ethical, theological, and lifestyle issues.

It is important to remember that creating a
church community for young adults does not always mean making them feel comfortable. Like all
Christians, young adults need and sometimes
even want to be challenged to live their Christian-
ity more faithfully. Jesus created an open space
into which the rich young man could enter life
and intimacy—"come, follow me"—but also issued

a difficult challenge—"go . . . sell what you pos-
sess and give to the poor."

Thus, while providing a safe, supportive arena
for exploring life's tough questions, the church
must also challenge young adults with a vision of
God's reign of shalom. (Shalom is a Hebrew word
meaning peace, well-being, wholeness, and har-
mony.) As young adults ask themselves whether
they will find meaning in making a buck and
looking out for number one, or in preparing for a
life of service, the church needs to be present to
lend guidance and support.

Second, the church can provide young adults
with a grounding community. Most young adults
want to belong. Ironically, however, young adulthood is often the time when people estrange
themselves from the church to look for intimacy
elsewhere. The reason for this separation is partly
due to the young adult's need to "push the
boundaries" a bit, but it is also due to the
church's failure to meet the intimacy needs of
young adults. Many churches unwittingly create
communities in which young adults simply do not
fit. Young adults begin to feel, then, that the
church has no relevance for their lives.

Granted, young adults are difficult to keep up
with. Their lives are often full of moves, changes,
and transitions. I am a member of a young adult
steering committee for my denomination. The
committee includes seven young adults and meets
about every four months. At every meeting, we
must publish a new list of addresses and telephone numbers, because one or more people on
the committee have moved, changed jobs, graduated from college, etc.

But there are several ways in which the church
may provide a home for young adults, whether
they are transient or settled. One of the churches
in the community where I attended college offered
a program called "Adopt a Student." Families in
the church would "adopt" a college student and
serve as her or his family away from home. The

student might join the family for Sunday dinner, a movie, or other outing.

Churches not located in a college community can easily adapt the "Adopt a Student" program. One possibility may be to assign a sponsor to each new young adult or young family that attends the church. The sponsor(s) would take care to include the new people, invite them to church activities, visit their homes, sit beside them in worship, etc.

Maintaining contact with young adults away from their home congregations is also important. One church displays pictures, names, and addresses of students, volunteer workers, and others who are away from home, urging members to write a letter or send a care package. Home congregations may also notify a church in the area where a young adult has relocated for schooling or a new job, so that church might make a contact with the young adult.

Mobile young adults can be invited to participate in the life of a congregation on a short-term basis. They can serve as preachers, worship leaders, or ushers. A musically gifted young adult may be asked to provide special music or fill in for the regular organist. A young adult may be asked to serve on a planning committee for a one-time event, such as a Christmas dinner or a Lenten worship series.

The church can offer special young adult Bible studies, activities and fellowship groups, but can also provide intergenerational events and programs. Young adults want and need community not only with "their own kind," but with the church as a whole. A young woman in my congregation recently expressed her excitement about the church's plans for an intergenerational vacation Bible school. She is even thinking about inviting some of her friends who have not been to church for a while.

The church can be a community where young adults find intimacy and identity. To accomplish

this, however, the church must afford opportunities for meaningful fellowship, it must provide
occasions to explore life and the Bible below the
surface, and it must invite young adults to serve
the church in a variety of ways.

Finally, the church can provide young adults
with charismatic leadership. Young adults do not
need "gurus" who will lead them by the nose like
so many sheep, but mentors who will take the
time and energy to develop a relationship and
help explore the important issues with which
young adults struggle.

I will never forget a campus pastor who listened
to my questions and fears, who allowed me to
cry, and who empowered me to make my own
decisions and be my own person. I am thankful
for seminary professors who took the time to help
me discern and nurture my gifts for ministry,
who helped me discover myself as a worthy, capable, and called woman of God. I thank God for
my parents and for the many Sunday school
teachers, friends, pastors and professors who
have demonstrated through their lives a vital, living, personal faith.

Sharon Parks further describes young adulthood as "the critical period for forming a
conviction of threshold existence and a passion
for the ideal." "Threshold existence" is living with
the sense that we were "made for more," that
there is more for us to "live into, embrace, or to
be embraced by," a sense that "we participate in
something wider and deeper than we have yet realized." I believe the rich young man in Matthew's
gospel story knew he was "made for more" than
just following the commandments and managing
his possessions. Nevertheless, he sorrowfully left
Jesus, uncertain that he could give up that which
prevented him from entering life. We can hope,
however, that after some earnest questioning and
reflection, the young man realized that Jesus had
offered him the very thing that he sought—wholeness, completeness, love, and belonging.

The Bible and Young Adult Ministry

Enten Eller

As we think about the Bible and young adult ministry, the perspective we take is important. More often than not, we have direct or indirect connections to church boards or decision-making bodies; from this perspective, we represent the establishment. Establishment is not a negative term; it is one that connotes those who are committed and dedicated to the church, those who support and help guide the church by our decisions and dedication.

From this perspective, we cannot approach young adults with the assumption that we will be able to minister *to* them in a patronizing sort of way. Not only are most young adults sensitive to this attitude as they make the transition away from home and into self-reliance, but both the Old and New Testaments give us a different model, that of ministry *with* those whom we seek to serve.

From the Old Testament we see God in relationship with the chosen people, interacting with them, listening to them, working with them, valuing them, enabling them to be channels of ministry to others. God's relationship to Moses is the epitome of this concept, although there are many other examples including Miriam, Abraham and Sarah, and many of the judges.

God continues this theme in the revelation of Jesus the Christ in the New Testament. Jesus said to the disciples, "I do not call you servants any longer . . . but I have called you friends" (John 15:15). True, Jesus worked at teaching the disciples, instructing them so they might learn the fullness of his mission, yet he also sent out the disciples on missions of their own, as partners. The disciples were not servants of Jesus, but with Jesus, fellow workers for the coming Reign of God.

One way to explore where young adult ministries may run into trouble regarding this concept of ministry *with* rather than *to* is the prophetic calling of the young Samuel in the third chapter of I Samuel. In this story, God calls the boy in the night. Samuel supposes it is his master Eli calling him, and so runs to Eli to see what he wants. After the second time that Samuel comes to Eli without being summoned, Eli realizes that it must be God calling Samuel and instructs him how to answer God next time. Sure enough, God calls once again and this time Samuel answers. Unfortunately, the news that God shares is very bad news for Eli. But the following morning Eli entreats Samuel to tell him the truth, and responds to the pronouncement from God with the words, "It is the Lord; let him do what seems good to him" (v. 18).

This biblical incident has much to say for young adult ministries. Like Eli, can those of us putting together young adult ministries accept and encourage those who hear a call, and not just pass it off as a pipe dream? Do we refuse to consider a vision just because those who present it are too young or don't really understand the situation at hand? How can we respond so as to help young adults grow in their own potential and join the church in ministry, as did Eli with Samuel, and Jesus with the disciples?

It is significant that Eli asks for the message Samuel has received from God, even though it is bad news, and in no way opposes Samuel for sharing what he has been given. It is incredible that Eli, representing the establishment (us, remember), is both willing and able to hear the voice of the younger generation that brings a word of criticism and judgment. Can we do the same? Can we set the next generation free to say what needs to be said without feeling responsible to edit, change, or condition the message?

As for criticism and judgment, young adults are well known for their inclination to stand over against the establishment on many fronts, and the arena of the church is no exception. Young adults who have visions often end up challenging the structures and the powers. This can create conflict and hard feelings, particularly when individuals who have dedicated much time and energy to the church (as we have) feel attacked.

But such conflicts are not foreign to our scriptures, either. Perhaps we can learn from what has been recorded before us. Take Daniel, and Shadrach, Meshach, and Abednego. In the book of Daniel, these Israelites were taken to a foreign land, young men chosen for a special service to the King, yet they felt that their principles were so important to them that they would risk their lives to keep themselves undefiled.

In the first chapter, this is not so risky a task, for it concerned what food they would eat. But by the third chapter of Daniel, these insolent, stubborn, intractable young adults (at least as viewed by the King and his advisors, the establishment of that day) were so unreasonable as to accept death in a fiery furnace rather than simply accommodate to the way things were in the system. Now, we all know that the story didn't end that way, but one point is nevertheless clear: dedication to principle and courage are a threat to power that is self-interested.

So what can we learn about young adults and young adult ministries from such a story? First, young adults are willing to buck the system, to stand up and say something for what they think is right, or against what they think is wrong. But more importantly, ministries working with young adults—and I dare say that such should include all facets of the church—will at times be presented with challenges. The key is to find some way of responding other than creating a fiery furnace! True, by the grace of God, through the furnace in Daniel (and that demonstration of faithfulness that challenged the system) good came: the King recognized the power of the true God and the glory of God was acknowledged throughout the kingdom.

In the same way, challenges to the church are often of vital importance to the community of faith, both as needed corrections and as calls to faithfulness, or simply as a way of raising awareness. Jesus, a representative of a "younger generation" to the church of his day, is by far the leading example of one who questioned and challenged, yet did so to show God's will more clearly to those who were concerned with being right with God. Then and now, the church or system that cannot tolerate protest is already showing signs of "dis-ease."

Furthermore, young adults may choose unconventional means to make a point or lodge a protest. Indeed, the church is sometimes frustrated with their creativity and their willingness to depart from the normal, staid conventions established in the church over the years. Take the story of Tamar and Judah from Genesis 38. Judah, the son of Israel, had gone against the law by refusing to give his youngest son to Tamar, the woman who was married to and outlived both his elder sons in turn. This was a serious matter, but Tamar had little recourse against the older, established male authority. With no other options, Tamar put on a veil to conceal her identity and waited by a crossroad where her father-in-law Judah was to pass. We don't know what Tamar had in mind, but when she was propositioned by Judah she accepted and became pregnant. When her pregnancy began to show three months later, Judah was told of his daughter-in-law's state and he condemned her to be burned for her adultery.

As she was taken off to be executed, however, Tamar sent proof that *he* was the baby's father. Judah responded, "She is more in the right than I, since I did not give her to my son Shelah" (v. 26).

Tamar used unorthodox means to get her point across! The message for us as we ponder young adult ministries is this: can we, as those representing the older generation, the establishment, those in power, be open to hear and understand the message to be shared, despite the medium? It is incredible that Judah, the older male with all the power and authority over Tamar, even control of her very life, was able to say, "She is more in the right than I." He was able to clearly see the issues at stake, rather than wielding power to suppress what confronted him. Can we do as well?

Returning to Daniel, Shadrach, Meshach, and Abednego, we must also look at the importance of peers as we try to understand the Bible and young adults. As one reads the first few chapters of Daniel, it isn't hard to form an image of Daniel as a model for the other three. Not only could Shadrach, Meshach, and Abednego follow the lead of Daniel's dedication, but they drew support from each other as peers committed together. Indeed, as we see clearly in the stories about David and Jonathan in I Samuel 18-20, often friends can assume such importance as to be closer than family. David and Jonathan made pacts with each other, took risks for each other, and covered for each other, even in defiance of Jonathan's father Saul, the King. There is no denying the close emotional bonds that tie young adults together.

As we understand young adults to be those for whom peers and friends are very important, it becomes clear that a group of strangers has very little chance of experiencing meaningful ministry together. Somehow an inviting core group needs to be found and nurtured, and means provided for the young adults to form friendships and ties that can be meaningful to them. The leadership, those who are willing to invest themselves in sowing relationships with young adults, will also reap a rich harvest in the process.

Another theme about young adults has also begun to surface through the biblical stories. Young adults, more often than their elders, exhibit the energy and commitment to doggedly follow what they think is right, despite many obstacles and hardships. The passages from Daniel bear this out, as does our discussion of Jesus, Tamar, and David and Jonathan. When this determination is coupled with a position that challenges the community of faith, difficulties can arise in the church, yet difficulties that hold much promise for the growth of the church in faithfulness and inner strength. But this dedication can also live itself out in a different way. For example, take the story of Esther.

Esther presents an interesting case. Here was a Jew who concealed her identity instead of holding out for what was right. Esther, in many senses of the words, gave up her body and soul. There were none of the vegetable-eating, idol-abhorring, stay-firm-unto-death antics of the three heros of the fiery furnace. Her cousin, Mordecai, refused to bow to Haman and so incurred his wrath. But, at Mordecai's instruction, Esther kept her background hidden until such a time as she had to steel her nerve and respond to a call like none she had faced before.

This strikes a chord with many young adults, who for one reason or another are unwilling to be different from those at their workplaces, unwilling to say much about their faith, and unwilling to be different from the crowd. Is this related to the desire to be accepted, to have friends, to be in a community of peers? After all, those desires can be characteristic of young adults. Yet many young adults may be like Esther, seemingly undedicated on the outside, but on the inside waiting for the right moment in which to take a stand, waiting for the time that calls forth their allegiance.

The challenge in young adult ministry is to be able to welcome those young adults who may still be dedicated in secret, or who go along with the crowd for a while. How also may we together provide a place where young adults can steel their nerves to meet the challenges that lie ahead? This is a question not at all unrelated to the one raised by the story of Gideon, found in Judges 6—8. Gideon ended up winning the battle, but at first he was scared, uncertain, testing. Afraid of being seen by day, he acted by night. Then, called to an even greater task, Gideon put out first one fleece and then another, worrying whether God really was calling him in this way.

This story raises the same questions as does the story of Esther, but also asks how we intend to make room in our young adult ministries for both the certainties as well as the uncertainties that we all have. Young adults are not only moving into a period of uncertainty in their lives, they do not have the luxury of many years' experience of resolving or learning to live the questions. How can young adult ministries acknowledge, accept, and assist in these complex challenges? Blocking the questions, or worse, providing simple, rigid answers, will only hinder the process.

"Living into the questions" is a theme for many young adults. Young adults often find themselves in a whirl of events, choices, and life-changing situations. An apt scriptural illustration is the story of Mary, the young mother of Jesus (see Luke 1:26-38). Thrust in an instant from singleness to pregnancy out of wedlock, trying to put together a home with her innocent husband-to-be, Mary is not without questions ("how can this be?") but is able to accept and live out life even in the face of this mystery. Indeed, the element of mystery is highly attractive to young adults these days. Mystery, however, cannot be created artificially by restricting information, or by presenting something yet-to-be-explained. Mystery must touch on the unfathomable, on the inexplicable God whose ways are higher than our ways, whose glory overshadows even our wildest imagination. It is this God who sent an angel to Mary, this God who was able to create life and then sustain it, both in this world as well as in Mary's womb. This is the genuine mystery that young adults seek.

The more practical considerations of Mary's story are not to be ignored, however. The church must train young adult leaders to respond to people who find themselves in awkward situations, like pregnancy, divorce, and addictions.

No discussion of young adults in scripture could be complete without mentioning the parable of the prodigal son, found in Luke 15:11-32. The classic tale of young adulthood, this story of the prodigal illuminates themes carried to young adults. The scripture identifies with young adults who are in search of themselves, seeking their fortunes, wanting to try to make it on their own, testing lifestyles and allegiances, trying on different roles, searching out dependable peers, testing different loyalties and value structures, and experiencing deep loneliness. The point, however, is not the condition of the prodigal, but that the one keeping the house actually welcomed the prodigal home with open arms! For a patriarch of that day to *run* after anyone was a scandal; to run after a good-for-nothing child (or so people thought) would be inconceivable! There were no questions, no cross-examinations, no conditions, no promises. Past experiences notwithstanding, the prodigal was welcomed home.

This means even more when one remembers that to come home is the hardest move: not even prophets are welcome in their own countries. Prodigals can always become converted somewhere else, and there be welcomed as those who have overcome a terrible past; but it is terrifying to return home where people know you, where people remember. For those of us who have stayed home, it may take a lot of courage to welcome home those we knew before, who "betrayed" us as they left.

The parable does not end with the welcome home. One more character enters, the dutiful son. Yes, what about those young adults who have always done what was asked of them? What about those young adults who may be enmeshed in the church in a way that calls forth their dedication and commitment without challenging them as individuals? How can our ministries feed those young adults before they end up like the dutiful son: discontented, burned out, feeling like they have been used, committed but unhappy?

Both children need to be welcomed home and offered love and acceptance. If not, both may end up leaving—the prodigal for the second time, the dutiful for the first—in search of a place that will become a new home.

Young Adults in the '90s

Steve Clapp

Most denominations define "young adults" as people between the ages of 18 and 35. Some churches lower the upper end to 30; and others, in light of the aging baby boomers, are tempted to raise it to 40. Within the 18 to 35 span, one encounters tremendous diversity. For example:

- Cheryl, 25 years old and single, who works as assistant manager of a clothing store.
- Andrew, 20 years old and single, who is a junior in college.
- Sarah, 21 years old and single, who is in the Air Force.
- Megan, 31 years old, who works as a salesperson for a large computer company and who is a single parent. Her daughter is three years old and is in a combination nursery school and day care while Megan is at work.
- Bob, 23 years old and single, who is about to start his first job as a high school teacher.
- Susan and Jim, both 28 years old, who are married and expecting the birth of their first child. Jim is an

attorney. Susan is a nurse and expects to take six months off after the birth of the child before returning to work.

- Carol, 29 years old, and Bruce, 32 years old, who have been married for seven years. They have three children, ages two, three, and six. Bruce is in a middle-management position in a large corporation. Carol occasionally substitute teaches, but finds most of her time consumed with the needs of the three young children.
- Hal, 24 years old and single, who is confined to a wheelchair by a disease he has had since birth. He received a degree in engineering and works as a technician in an electronics firm.
- Sally, 19 years old, and Ben, 22 years old, who have been married for three years. Neither of them has a high school degree. They have two children, and number three is on the way. Sally does child care in their home, and Ben works at a garage.

Young adults constitute a significant part of the population, and they are an extremely diverse group. Obviously no single program or emphasis at the local church level will reach and attract all the young adults just described. In 1991, the oldest young adults (35 years of age) were born in 1956; the youngest (18 years of age) were born in 1973. There are tremendous differences in the settings into which the oldest and the youngest were born, and there are deeper differences between these young adults and older adults in the church. The oldest young adults can remember things that happened in connection with the Vietnam War, for example, while the youngest cannot. Even the oldest young adults, however, will not have any first-hand memories of World War II.

The U.S. Census Bureau shares the following information on age distribution in the United States, including actual figures for 1960 and 1990 and projections for 2030 based on current death rates:

Age	1960	1990	2030
Under 18	35.7%	25.8%	21.9%
18-24	8.9	10.3	11.6
25-34	12.7	17.4	12.3
35-44	13.4	15.2	13.0
45-54	11.4	10.2	12.1
55-64	8.6	8.4	8.4
65 and older	9.3	12.7	20.7

Adding the figures for 18-24 and 25-34 gives totals of 21.6 percent for 1960, 27.7 percent for 1990, and 23.9 percent projected for 2030. The number of young adults has increased significantly in the past 30 years, and even though there will be a gradual decline by 2030, they will continue to be a significant percentage of the population.

Much has been written about the baby boomers. In 1991, the baby boomers are those people between 27 and 45 years of age; thus some of them are no longer in the young adult years. By the year 2000, the baby boomers will be between 36 and 54 years of age, no longer young adults. As we think about work with young adults, it's important to keep in mind some of the characteristics of the baby boomers, but it's also important to remember that they are, like everyone else, getting older!

Popular music, television (including cable channels and MTV), and motion pictures have very much influenced this age group. That is especially true for the young adults between 18 and 24 years of age. In creating programs that will effectively reach young adults, the church needs to keep in mind how much young adults have been influenced by those media and how attractive those media are to many of them. Most young

adults have grown up in a world that in some
ways seems smaller and less diverse than the
world of their parents and grandparents. The
same restaurants, stores, theaters, and television
programs are found across the United States and,
in many instances, around the world. Even local
television newscasters seem to look like those in
other parts of the country and to use a format
almost identical to those at stations hundreds of
miles away. On the other hand, the apparent
shrinking of the world also means that today's
young adults have often been exposed to more
ethnic diversity than their parents were, and that
they have a greater understanding of events in
other parts of the world.

Young adults themselves represent a tremendous   diversity.   One   of   their   common
characteristics, unfortunately from the perspective
of the Christian community, is that they are less
likely than older adults to be active within the life
of a church. Interestingly, they are not necessarily
less likely to believe in God, to pray, or to have
made commitments to Christ. Many of them,
however, have not found their faith drawing them
to the institutional church.

It is particularly important to remember that
young adults are searching for intimacy. In a
1988 study that compared young adults active in
the church with those inactive or not members of
a church, it was found that:

- Young adults both inside and outside the
  church express a longing to grow closer to
  God and to understand what is really important in life.
- Young adults are more likely than older
  adults to express loneliness, a sense of isolation, a need for meaningful companionship.
- Young adults are actively seeking to better
  understand themselves and to improve the
  way in which they relate to others.
- Young adults who are active in a church are
  more likely than older adults in the church

to say that a significant part of their social needs are met by the Christian community. Young adults who are not active in a church or are not members of a church report that they do not feel it likely that their social needs will be met within a church.

The study on which the above information is based (Wesley Kolbe Publishing, Peoria, Illinois) makes it clear that the search for intimacy with God and with other people is of special concern to young adult. Effective outreach to them depends in large part on recognizing that need.

We sometimes think of the word "intimacy" as referring primarily to the relationship between a man and a woman in marriage or a close sexual relationship outside of marriage. The meaning of the word as used here and elsewhere in this book, however, is broader. Intimacy refers to the closeness of one's relationships with others. We can have intimate relationships with people our own age, with younger people, and with older people. Intimate relationship bring a sense of trust and confidence, the ability to be honest about ourselves and to feel loved and accepted.

In *Intimacy: The Longing of Every Human Heart*, Terry Hershey shares the observation that "each one of us desires closeness at the same time that we protect ourselves from it" (p. 22). We desperately want to be closer to others, but we can be threatened by seeming to expose too much of ourselves to others. Thus the church needs to offer intimacy to young adults, but it must do so in a way that avoids being pushy or threatening. "Instant intimacy" is simply not possible. Intimacy must be built over a period of time. The church at its best does an excellent job of accomplishing that as people have opportunities to study together, worship together, and work together.

In the years ahead, the need for intimacy by young adults may grow as today's teenagers mature. Many youth workers are very concerned about the frequency with which teenagers suffer

from depression, profound loneliness, and sometimes suicidal tendencies. Suicide, in fact, has
emerged as a significant cause of death among
today's teenagers. Most teens who have major
problems with depression have failed to achieve
the intimacy they crave with their parents, other
significant adults, and friends their own age. The
unmet need for intimacy by these teenagers continues to afflict many of them as young adults.

Young Adults and Work

Young adults have had to deal with a significant expansion of the formal training process. As
the technological sophistication of society has increased, the need for training beyond high school
has also grown. Tremendous numbers of young
adults enroll in colleges, universities, and trade
schools. Others enter the armed forces and receive vocational training there.

Many of today's young adults are far more comfortable with computers and related technology
than older adults. Young adults who are in college very likely use computers as part of the
study process, and young adults in the work
place are likely to use computers and to be comfortable doing so. They are less likely than older
adults to be offended by the extent to which government agencies and businesses maintain
personal information on computer and exchange
it.

The United States and Canada have become in-
creasingly mobile countries over the past 50
years, with more and more people making fre-
quent moves for improved vocational
opportunities. Young adults have often grown up
with parents who made moves for vocational reasons, and many of them take it for granted that
one moves when necessary. They are less likely to
have strong roots in one community from their
childhood or to have as strong a connection to a
childhood church as are older adults.

Although some studies show exceptions, in general young adults want to get ahead financially every bit as much as older adults. Some of them are even more ambitious and consider themselves failures if they have not achieved considerable financial success by the age of 30. Other young adults, though sharing the dreams of their successful contemporaries, are barely able to earn enough to get by.

The tremendous increase in the percentage of women in the work force affects all age groups but especially young adults. Here's how the U.S. Census Bureau identifies women as a percentage of the work force:

Year	Total	Married	Widowed/ Divorced	Single
1890	18.9%	13.9%	17.9%	68.2%
1940	27.4	36.4	15.1	48.5
1987	56.0	54.7	19.4	25.9

Note that in 1890, over two-thirds of the women in the work force were single. By 1987, only 25.9 percent of the women in the work force were single. Women have moved from composing less than one-fifth of the work force to over half of the work force in the United States.

The reality of women in the work force is even more striking for women under the age of 35. Over two-thirds of the women with children work outside the home. Over half of those return to work before the baby's first birthday.

In the vast majority of households, the combination of a high cost of living and the desire for a high standard of living have resulted in both husbands and wives working especially among young adult couples. The fact that both husband and wife work when there are small children at home has two very important implications for the church. First, the provision of nursery school and day care has become an important potential form of ministry and a way to attract young adults to the life of the church. Second, it means that the total responsibilities of husband and wife are enormous. The tendency of couples to return to church when the first child is born is true but not to as great an extent as a few years ago. Part of the reason is that not even church can attract a husband and wife who are tired from the pressures of working and parenting by Sunday morning.

Sexuality and Marriage

Young adults are likely to differ significantly from older adults in their attitudes toward sexuality and marriage. There have always been differences between generations, and the extent of those differences has never been greater than today. According to the Wesley Kolbe survey:

• Young adults are much more likely than older adults to feel that there is nothing wrong with premarital intercourse providing neither party is manipulated. Acceptance of premarital intercourse has grown over the last several years, and that acceptance is especially great among young adults who are single. Gallup polls and other surveys reflect the same reality.

• Those who are single, active in the church, and also sexually active feel that they cannot be open about their sexual activity in conversations with people in the church. Many feel the need to "cover up" the fact that they live with another person without benefit of marriage. A large number of young adults stay away from the church because of the "judgmental attitude" they feel older church members have about sexual activity.

• Young adults are more likely than older adults to feel that abortion may be the best of bad options under some circumstances.

There are many older adults who agree with them, but not by the same proportion.

- Young adults who have gone through a divorce feel that their divorced status will be a barrier to close relationships with others in a church. Those who were members of a church at the time of their divorce feel, almost without exception, that the church was not very supportive of them during the process.

Today's young adults have matured during a time of radical changes in societal attitudes toward sexuality and marriage, so it is not surprising that their values in this area differ from those of many older people in the church. Contraceptive devices have been widely available, social prohibitions about premarital sex have been relaxed, and abortion has been more readily, legally available.

Since 1929, according to the U.S. Census Bureau, the marriage rate has remained relatively constant while the divorce rate has tripled. People are also waiting somewhat longer before marriage. In 1960, the median age at the time of first marriage for women was 20.5 and for men was 22.5. In 1985, the figure for women was 23.5 and for men was 26.

Increasing numbers of young adults choose to remain single, and some of those who remain single do have children. Single parents are more likely to be missing from the church than any other category of young adults, which stands in marked contrast to the fact that married couples with children are the ones most likely to be involved in the church. There are also increasing numbers of unmarried couple households. In 1970, according to the Census Bureau, there were half a million unmarried couple households. By 1988, that number had increased to 2.6 million including 800,000 with children. Most unmarried households are made up of young adults.

The nature of home life has changed radically with so many husbands and wives working. There is enormous evidence that women are the ones doing most of the child care and household work even when both husband and wife work the same number of hours. *Utne Reader* (March/April, 1990) estimates that over the course of a year, wives work a month of 24-hour days more than their husbands! Husbands come home to watch television while their wives do the cleaning, cooking, and caring for the children. In a 1990 study by George Levinger of 600 couples who filed for divorce, the number two reason given for seeking a divorce by women was "neglect of home or children" by the husband. (The number one reason continues to be the broad category of "mental cruelty," claimed by the husband, wife, or both.) These realities are even more true for young adult couples than for older adults, and the divorce rate of young adults with children is exceptionally high.

Young adults have also matured during a time of tremendous emphasis on physical fitness and personal appearance. While "looks" have always been important in society, concern about them has reached the point of obsession for many people. Men and women differ in how they feel about their appearance. According to the November/December 1990 issue of *Health* magazine, 68 percent of men like how they look when naked; only 22 percent of women feel the same way. Interestingly, the Wesley Kolbe study found that 73 percent of young adult men liked their physical appearance in contrast to 39 percent of young adult women. Thus young adults seem slightly more likely than older adults to feel good about their appearance, but a significant gap is present between how men and women feel about themselves in that regard.

Multiculturalism, Politics, and Activism

In working with young adults, it's extremely important to recognize that the young adult population includes increasing percentages of Hispanics, Asians, and African Americans. In recent years, significant numbers of people have immigrated to the United States from Mexico and from Asia. Some of the immigrants are themselves young adults; others have had children who have become young adults. Birth rates have been somewhat higher for African Americans than for whites, with the result that the percentage of young adults who are black has increased.

The predominantly white congregation that builds a young adult ministry without considering the possible presence of other ethnic groups in the community will be missing a rich source of members. Some of those from ethnic cultures have differing religious traditions. Many Asians are Buddhists and thus may be difficult to interest in the Christian community. Hispanics tend to be Christian; 70 percent have been brought up Catholic and around 18 percent Protestant. Some communities have large Native American populations.

Efforts to identify the political persuasion of young adults are doomed to failure. Much has been said about the "new conservationism" present in many young adults. On the other hand, there are significant numbers of young adults who solidly identify with more liberal political traditions and resist the innate conservatism of many congregations. Then there are young adults who are so frustrated by the inability of government leaders and political figures to solve the problems of society that they have chosen to characterize themselves as "non-political." In general, efforts at programming that assume a particular political orientation on the part of young adults are not likely to be successful. Young adults have the same diversity as older members of the congregation.

Although they are not more (or less) political than older adults, young adults are more likely to want to make a difference in society. They are, on the whole, more idealistic than older adults and more likely to be attracted to programs that they feel will help families, children, the homeless, or the hungry. They are especially interested in programs that further world peace. This represents a tremendous opportunity for the church.

Religious Practices and Attitudes

While young adults are less likely than older adults to be active in a church, they are very likely to believe in God and to have strong religious interests and concerns. The Wesley Kolbe study asked young adults who were not involved in a local church if they would consider participation in a Bible study group that had an "accepting and affirming" atmosphere, and a whopping 48 percent said that they would! They reported strong interest in the Bible but also concern that they feel supported and helped by a group rather than made to feel judged and foolish. They also do not want to be put on the spot to share their opinions.

Gallup polls have consistently shown that Americans have a greater interest in the Bible than a willingness to actually study it. Young adults are no exception to the rule, but their level of curiosity is actually slightly higher than that of older adults, according to the Wesley Kolbe study. Bible study groups offer excellent potential for outreach to young adults.

Two-thirds of the baby boomers dropped out of organized religion. In recent years, over one-third have returned. Of those returning, 60 percent are married with children. Those baby boomers least likely to return are married couples who do not have children or single people who do not have children. Similar trends are present among the younger group of young adults.

In a cover article on the return of baby boomers to the church, the December 17, 1990, issue of *Newsweek* pointed out that baby boomers "inspect congregations as if they were restaurants and leave if they find nothing to their taste." The Wesley Kolbe study found that same reality to be true not of baby boomers but also of other young adults. Denominational loyalty is much lower for young adults than it was for their parents and grandparents. In the Wesley Kolbe study, 78 percent of the Protestants said that they would change denominations if they found a church of a different denomination that better met their needs. Perhaps even more surprising, 40 percent of the Catholics in that study indicated that they would change to a Protestant church if doing so would result in better programs and opportunities for themselves or their children.

Some young adults actually belong to or participate in more than one congregation. It's especially common for young singles to continue to hold membership and worship in their parents' church but to participate in a young adult study group or social group at another church.

There is a growing tendency in both the United States and Canada for people to see the church serving *them* as individuals and families rather than to see the church as a means for serving *God*. That difference in perspective has a profound impact on the life of the church. While that view is true to some extent for many adults, it is strikingly true for young adults. Yet those same young adults have a strong need to make a difference in the lives of other people and of society, and the church can provide that kind of service opportunity.

Why do young adults leave the church? The Wesley Kolbe study, Gallup polls, and other studies identify some key factors:

- Some young adults feel that the church is more concerned about itself as an organization than about meeting spiritual needs. They often feel that the church puts too much emphasis on raising money for its own institutional needs.
- Some young adults feel that they can meet their spiritual need just as well on their own as through a church. Many feel that the church's teachings and beliefs are too narrow.
- Some young adults acknowledge simply drifting away from the church, getting out of the habit, without being especially happy or unhappy with the church.
- Some young adults feel that the church doesn't really care whether or not they are involved.
- Some young adults feel that older church members will judge them negatively because of differences in attitudes toward sex and marriage. Many likewise feel that the church's teachings on sex and marriage are too narrow.
- Some young adults have been offended or hurt by something that happened in church.
- Some young adults leave the church because of bad preaching or a bad experience with a particular minister.

The more important question for our purpose, of course, is: What factors bring young adults back to the church? The Wesley Kolbe study identified these major reasons given by young adults who had been nonmembers or inactive members and who then became actively involved:

1. More than any other single factor, young adults said that they returned to church involvement because someone invited them to do so and showed a genuine interest in them.

2. The second factor in importance was the birth of a first child. Young adult couples felt a strong need and obligation to return to the

church when they became parents. It is important to note, however, that this did not hold true for young adults who were single parents, because those people felt they would not be well accepted in the church.

3. The third factor was that a particular minister or church staff member showed a positive interest in them or exhibited a style of ministry that made them feel the church could be more relevant to their lives.

4. The fourth factor, almost equal to the third, was that the young adults felt a strong inner need to learn more about God and to deepen their ties to God through church involvement.

Note that the first and third factors both focus on the role of one or more people in inviting the young adults to become involved or having a positive impact on them. In *The People's Religion*, George Gallup, Jr. and Jim Castelli make an interesting observation about the boom in church attendance and involvement that took place in the United States during the fifties: "A remarkable 24 percent of American adults said that at some time in 1957 they had called on people to ask them to attend or join their church. And as many as 60 percent said they had been called upon to attend or join a church" (p. 9). Much of the reason for the great success of the institutional church in the 1950s may well be found in the willingness of people to visit others and invite them to be active in the Christian community.

This book offers many creative program ideas and insights into understanding young adults. All that information, however, will only be useful as people who are active in the church reach out to young adults, helping them discover the difference that Jesus Christ and involvement in Christ's body—the church—can make in their lives.

Framework for Young Adult Ministry

Steve Clapp

The introduction and the three chapters that follow it have attempted to provide a biblical and theological perspective on young adult ministry and to help you better understand young adults in the nineties. We now move to chapters offering practical guidance for young adult ministry.

As you work to improve your church's outreach to young adults, think in terms of establishing a special young adult task force, committee, or leadership team to take an overall look at young adult needs in your church and community and to coordinate the efforts of various individuals and groups. This team could be as few as three people or as many as a dozen, depending on the size of your congregation and community. Be sure to have people of young adult age included in this group, even if that means recruiting people who have been inactive in the church or who are not yet members. If your minister or another staff member is not a member of the committee, maintain careful communi-

cation with that person or persons since staff support will be important to the success of your efforts.

The following principles or guidelines for your efforts at reaching young adults more effectively are all expanded in the chapters that follow:

1. Help your congregation develop more open, accepting attitudes toward young adults. If you successfully reach more young adults for your church, there will be some differences in values between those people and older members of the congregation. An open, accepting attitude on the part of older members will be a great help and will avoid driving away the young adults you've just gained. (See "Becoming an Open Congregation.")

2. Involve young adults in every possible phase of church leadership. A special young adult task force committee or leadership team is a good beginning; but your church as a whole won't become sufficiently sensitive or attractive to young adults until young adults have broad representation in organizations, boards, and committees of the church. It is especially important to have young adults represented in the top decision-making bodies of your church and on the personnel or pastor parish group. (See "Young Adults in Church Leadership.")

3. Make a concerted effort to regain young adults who belong to your church or have been loosely affiliated with your church but who have become inactive. This isn't an easy task! Reaching inactives can be more frustrating than reaching young adults who have not been connected with your church in the past. It is, however, a very important and rewarding task. These are also the young adults whom your church can most readily identify. Your young adult leadership group or others recruited for the task will need to make personal contact with these inactive young adults to learn from them and to gain new involvement from them. (See "Regaining Inactives.")

4. Develop a program to reach new young adults, people in the community who have not been connected with your church in the past. You'll find that the most direct route to these people is through young adults already in your church and through older adult members who have contact with young adults at work, in community organizations, and in neighborhoods. Coming to understand the needs of young adults in your community will help you do a more effective job developing new programs, services, and ministry opportunities. (See "Reaching New Young Adults.")

5. Develop new programs or find creative ways to involve single young adults in the life of your church. Single young adults are often frustrated by the fact that so many churches assume a strong family orientation in their planning. Thus young singles can feel left out or that they are an afterthought in the overall life of the church family. Find ways to include them either through new groups or organizations or through better integration into existing groups. (See "Singles in a Family World.")

6. Recognize the ways in which family life is different for many young adults today than it was a few years ago. Come to better understand the realities of both parents working, single parent households, and the widespread use of day care and nursery facilities. Develop programs that will reach married young adults and single young adults with children. (See "The Changing Nature of Marriage and Family.")

7. Begin new groups and programs that will meet the needs of the various young adults in your church and community. You won't be able to successfully start many groups or programs at one time, but you can target specific needs of young adults and begin new groups with strategies that almost guarantee success. (See "Starting New Groups.")

8. Help staff members cultivate attitudes and styles of ministry that will encourage young adult participation in the church. While having a staff member who is himself or herself a young adult can certainly help, age isn't as important a factor as openness, warmth, and good follow-through with members and potential members. (See "Staffing for Young Adult Growth.")

9. Obtain print and media resources that will help you establish meaningful young adult programs. Many excellent resource materials are available. There are also people and agencies who can provide you with helpful information and insight. (See "Resources.")

Becoming an Open Congregation

Karen Peterson Miller

Whether or not we are prepared to journey with young adults, the people of God have been instructed from the beginning of creation to nurture and to care for one another. It is the responsibility of the whole church to engage in an open, flexible style of ministry with young adults. And it is essential that those of us who have moved beyond the experiences of young adulthood remember what it was like to be involved in a variety of religious and secular activities in order that we might be gentle, loving, and caring in our understanding of young adults who are almost always in motion.

Part of maturing and developing for the young adult is the search for a mate, a career, a profession, a place of belonging, and meaning in life. Young adults want to establish themselves as participants in a life of vitality and wholeness. What the church must do is encourage and nurture young adults in their journeys so that they become a part of our faith communities. The call for the church in assimilating young adults is to be faithful in assisting the young adults to be the whole people God created them to be as their lives evolve.

In trying to determine what it means to become an open congregation, a serious look needs to be taken at what the church has done to create an exclusive, non-accepting attitude toward young adults. In the next few pages, the description of Jane and her experience in the church will invite you to ponder where your congregation is or may have been in relationship to nurturing and creating a healthy climate for young adults.

Each congregation is unique, and the kind of openness that evolves can only be determined by the willingness of congregations to change or mend their ways with the hope that young adults can be a vital part of ministry. The words of the prophet Hosea provide an image of encouragement as we prepare to minister with young adults.

When Israel was a child,
    I loved him,
and out of Egypt I called
    my son.

The more I called them,
    the more they went from me;
they kept sacrificing to the Baals,
    and offering incense to idols.

Yet it was I who taught Ephraim
    to walk,
I took them up in my arms;
but they did not know that I
    healed them.

I led them with cords of human
    kindness,
with bands of love.

I was to them like those
    who lift infants to their cheeks.

> I bent down to them and fed
> them.
> Hosea 11:1-4

As you read about Jane and her experiences with the church, keep in mind that this is not an exceptional situation, nor is it any different from what some of us may have experienced in the church. Sharing Jane's story is to remind the church that ministry needs to be open, inclusive, and sharing rather than exclusive. Ponder each aspect of the story with the idea that a major change must occur in most congregations in order to assimilate young adults into the life of the whole church.

Jane is 30 years old and single. She has been in the same geographical region, small town, and church all of her life. The church records state that she has belonged to The Community Church from the day of her birth. However, there was a span of five years (ages 24-29) in which Jane did not attend the church of her birth, childhood, adolescence, and young adulthood.

When Jane left The Community Church, she did so for the following reasons:

1. The sermons and the worship experience had little relevance for Jane.

2. Jane was more than a daughter of one of the outstanding families in the church and community, she was a person in her own right and yet she seldom felt acceptance as her own person.

3. Many of her peers were involved elsewhere and she had few people her own age with whom to relate.

4. Older adults in the congregation paid very little attention to Jane and even thought she was a bit peculiar.

5. Jane felt very lonely at The Community Church.

6. There were no invitations to be part of the leadership of the church.

7. Jane was shy and reserved, so starting and sustaining conversations with others was difficult.

8. The Community Church did not have a young adult ministry and she was not one to take initiative to get one started.

9. Jane was curious to find out about life in other congregations and other kinds of institutions or social events.

10. Sunday morning was a good time to claim distance and space from her family and an opportunity to sleep and to relax.

Take a few minutes to think carefully and thoughtfully about Jane. In what way do you think the congregation that you are a part of helps to contribute to the feelings that Jane developed? Can you name those individuals who are no longer in your congregation who are between the ages of 20-35? Write those names down on paper and list beside each name any of the reasons for those people you have listed.

Through careful consideration it is hoped that congregations can reverse the feelings many young adults have about the church and can begin to create openness, flexibility, trust and caring for young adults. Perhaps congregations can then develop specific strategies for including young adults in the life of the church.

In order to think through a strategy for ministry with young adults, the whole congregation must have an increased sensitivity and awareness of how young adults feel when they are at the church. Naming a positive direction is simply a first step for the congregation. The difficult work starts with finding individuals who will commit themselves to developing relationships with and programs for young adults. Once again, reasons will be listed as a method for helping congregations to focus their energies on specific ways of developing a faith community where all young adults are accepted.

Sermons and the worship experience must have relevance for young adults. It is critical and necessary for the worship time and the sermon to have a life-application emphasis. A young adult needs to find encouragement, hope, and direction from the worship experience. Simply to be in church is seldom enough to keep a young adult interested and active in the life of the congregation. Frequently, what young adults look for in the sermon is a connection between the religious realm and everyday life.

Each person is a unique individual and yearns for acceptance of the person God has created him or her to be. Congregations must be willing to learn or to know and to love people for who they are becoming as they mature and develop. Young adults are in an intense process of self-discovery as well as self-doubt: Each young adult needs to be known and loved for who he or she is becoming as a precious child of God.

A congregation must be aware of the age range of young adults. Often, there are few young adults in any particular congregation. This means that a congregation must intentionally create one-to-one relationships with young adults. A way must be found to care for the young adults regardless of the age differences in the congregation. This is the opportunity to establish a mentoring relationship in which a specific person is chosen to be a mentor to a young adult. Helping young adults to find mentors in the congregation is extremely beneficial in strengthening the ties of a young adult to a congregation.

The role of a mentor can remove the barrier that is created in a small church where there are few young adults. A mentor can provide stability and guidance, and can share in hearing about the struggles or accomplishments of a young adult. Being with the young adult in the ups and downs of ordinary life is one of the tasks of a mentor. Mentors are encouraged to be in touch with the young adult on a weekly basis and to pursue relating with the young adult when not in worship or at church.

Older adults in the congregation need to learn that it is important to acknowledge a person's presence. When was the last time you noticed one of the young adults standing off to side of the sanctuary, narthex, or fellowship hall? Most likely, you have seen a young adult or two in that place Sunday after Sunday. Older adults (those people who have been with the church for decades) need to take initiative in approaching young adults. Many young adults feel that the church members care very little about them as young adults and even think that they are peculiar. Often, other church members leave the young adults to be by themselves rather than making inquiry into their lives. Perhaps long-term members might be surprised at the response of a young adult who is invited to brunch or lunch following worship. Usually, a meal provides a good opportunity to become acquainted.

Young adults feel lonely at church. For many young adults the church is a lonely place because of the emphasis on the family or people who have known each other for a long time. It is essential that, beginning with the pastor, a sincere, genuine, honest spirit of receiving young adults is created. Accepting a person as important and expressing delight in seeing that person is part of our responsibility as people of faith.

This is more than a "good morning and a handshake." A young adult needs to be engaged in a meaningful encounter that eases loneliness as well as aloneness.

Young adults are capable of providing leadership in the congregation. When young adults are asked to get involved, the response is quite often a positive one. But the young adult will need to be invited to enter into a leadership opportunity. Usually congregations hesitate to ask young adults to consider leadership responsibilities due to their mobility. However, young adults will commit themselves to leadership as long as the expectations are clearly stated. Young adults have many skills to offer that can be useful in terms of administration, finances, and long-range planning. Remember, it is the young adults who are most likely receiving the current training in our high-tech society. Also, young adults will commit themselves more easily to short-term tasks such as one month of Sunday school teaching, one week of vacation Bible school, six weeks of a Thursday night Bible study, etc. Keep working at new ways to include the young adults in leadership.

Budget and plan for a young adult ministry as an active, vital part of the congregation's growth and ministry in the community. Young adults will seldom take the initiative to ask for budget and staff to begin a young adult ministry. A congregation moving toward the 21st century needs to be oriented toward the future. Out of necessity, congregations need to provide money, programming, and staff for young adults. All too frequently young adults are expected to participate in whatever is offered, and it is difficult for young adults to relate to some of the more traditional opportunities found in a congregation.

Developing and providing relevant programs for young adults is essential. Organizing educational, spiritual, and personal experiences for young adults related to issues such as sexuality, loneliness, singleness, careers, parenting, and financial planning will help them realize the church is serious about nurturing their development. The church must be willing to trust the young adults to explore issues that are of the greatest concern to them as they explore the future.

Curiosity about other religious experiences and social opportunities will lead young adults to a process of discovery and the church needs to accept the

**mobility as well as the flexibility that is prevalent
among young adults.** Young adults will search for
activities and people who will help them to develop
and mature. There are many interesting programs
offered through community agencies and other faith
communities. The church need not be threatened
by the curiosity of young adults, as long as each
congregation provides a strong center from which
the young adult may search. It is important for the
young adult to experience differences as well as
similarities among all of God's people; therefore, a
congregation needs to adapt to the inquisitive, curious nature of young adults while letting them know
they are needed in the faith community.

**Young adults need to establish separateness and
independence.** All too often older adults criticize
young adults for becoming detached from the family
or the church family. What needs to be highlighted
and emphasized is that part of growing up and
maturing in the midst of a growing faith experience
is to differentiate and assert one's independence.
Young adults will want to do this and it is important for the congregation to understand this
behavior.

After considering Jane's experience with the church
and thinking about the kind of congregation that
might emerge as a congregation in which young
adults will grow and develop, where do you see your
congregation willing to make changes? In what way
can you help to facilitate the development of an
open, caring, nurturing congregation where people
like Jane are accepted, included, loved, and known?

A congregation only becomes all that it is in-
tended to be when individuals are willing to become
all that God has created them to be in relationship
to one another. Remember, young adults are in formation, on a journey, and the church can
encourage them to find space as well as to claim
an identity within a congregation while on the journey. Let us go into the 21st century with hope and
energy to make our congregations open, receptive
places of belonging for future generations.

Young Adults In Church Leadership

Steve Clapp

First Church has almost 200 members, but very few of them are young adults. Pam and Jeff are among that small number. They are in their mid-twenties and have been in the church for a little over two years. Pam teaches at a community high school, and Jeff is an accountant. They've enjoyed their membership in the church but have recently begun to feel frustrated. They've been the junior high youth group sponsors most of those two years and have also taught Sunday school for high school students. Both of them are on the church's education board.

Now they want to change the nature of their activity because they are a little burned out on the youth work and have just had their first child. They've agreed to continue teaching the Sunday school class, but they are no longer going to continue as junior high sponsors. They are uncomfortable because the pastor and a couple of church members applied considerable pressure trying to keep them from resigning as junior youth sponsors.

They didn't realize that they had made a lifetime commitment to that group!

Pam doesn't feel she can continue to serve on a board or committee of the church along with Jeff because child care usually isn't available for meetings. They both resigned the education board, but Jeff indicated that he would like to serve on the finance board or the trustee board. The church's nominating committee, however, didn't see it the same way and asked him to serve on the missions board. That's all right with Jeff, but he's observed that no one younger than 50 seems to be acceptable as a member of the finance board or the trustees. That seems especially strange to him since he's a certified public accountant and feels that he has a great deal to offer in those areas.

First Church has made some major errors in the relationship with Pam and Jeff. Those errors are common in many churches and sometimes act as serious barriers to young adult involvement. Tenure for any position in the church should be clearly specified, and people shouldn't be made to feel guilty for resigning from positions. Child care needs to be available during most regular meetings and programs of the church. Churches need to free themselves from preconceptions about who should be youth workers, trustees, and other officers.

Successful young adult ministry generally takes place in parishes that involve young adults in every phase of decision making. Token involvement of young adults just is not sufficient. While you may not have enough available young adults at the present to use them as extensively as you wish, it is very important to give careful consideration to where they are used and to develop leadership recruitment strategies that will help you increase the number of young adults who are involved.

A church can't develop sensitivity to the needs of people like Pam and Jeff (or to the young sin-

gles and young adult couples without children)
unless young adults are active enough to present
their opinions and needs in decision-making
groups of the church. Here are some strategies to
help you better involve young adults in church
leadership:

1. Identify the young adults who are already in
leadership positions in the church. Consult these
young adults about church leadership needs. The
active young adults can share valuable insights
on barriers to participation that may affect others.
They are also the best source for the names of
other young adults who are potential leaders in
the church.

2. Have clear job descriptions and clear tenure
for every leadership position in the church. Any
person considering a position as teacher, officer,
counselor, or committee member—whether that
person is 25 years old or 65 years old—needs
that information. Many people refuse to accept
positions simply because they do not understand
what is required and fear that they will be inadequate for the task. None of us wants to fail, and
young adults may be especially sensitive to feelings of inadequacy because of more limited
experience in the church than older adults. Having clear job descriptions helps people understand
their responsibilities and makes it more likely
that they will agree to accept positions. Clear tenure statements let people know they are not
accepting an eternal position. It's fine to let people renew at the end of a term, but they should
clearly be asked if they want to continue. When
people have served in a position and want to re-
sign, that wish should always be respected.

3. Consider the use of vice-chairpersons or
"leaders in preparation" for some boards or committees in your church. Many people who will
refuse to be chairperson of a group because of
concern over the expectations involved will readily
agree to be vice-chairperson or to be a "leader in
preparation." That provides one year to learn

about the board or committee and to observe how another person handles the coordination of the group. Then it becomes much easier for the vice-chairperson to become chairperson of the group in the next term.

4. Hold an annual leadership seminar or leadership retreat designed to train present and potential leaders. Make the event an honor in your church, and invite young adults who are potential leaders to participate. The seminar or retreat design should include:

- Bible study and spiritual growth opportunities.
- Background on your denominational heritage and structure. This is especially important for young adults who often choose a church on factors other than denominational identity. Once in the church, they'll feel more comfortable knowing something about the denomination.
- Information on congregational structure and organization. Help people know how decisions are made, what group has the final authority, what the role of the minister is, and how funding is arranged.
- Provide information on healthy leadership styles for the church. Working with church volunteers differs significantly from working in a secular organization, and most leaders need help understanding those distinctions.

The above leadership material can be covered easily in a retreat setting, which also gives people an opportunity to interact informally. If you use a seminar approach, then you will need four to six evenings to cover the material. Your denomination should have resources that can be used in such a seminar or retreat setting.

5. Use membership orientation and study groups to identify potential young adult leaders. Ask those who provide leadership to these groups to be alert for young adults who show interest and should be contacted by the church's nomi-

nating committee. Membership orientation groups are very different for new members and need to provide enough background about your church to help new members feel comfortable.

6. Expose faulty assumptions that are barriers to young adult involvement. Faulty assumptions obviously hurt Pam and Jeff at First Church and similar problems could well exist in your church. Consider these faulty assumptions:

- "Men make better trustees than women, and older adults are more responsible than younger adults." NO! Women are as competent as men to be trustees, and young adults like Jeff have a great deal to offer.
- "Young adults make the best youth advisors." NOT NECESSARILY! Young adults can make excellent youth group advisors, but middle-aged and older adults can also do an outstanding job. Simply being young doesn't guarantee a good understanding of teenagers. While you may well wish to use young adults with youth groups, don't make the mistake of stereotyping the young adults or the teenagers.
- "Women are better than men in leading the nursery, preschool, and elementary classes of the church school." NO! Men have much to give children and can deeply enjoy the contact with them. Many young couples will enjoy working together with children, and the male contact is especially valuable for children who may be growing up in single parent homes with a mother but no father.
- "Young adults aren't as concerned as older adults about spiritual matters and the Bible." NO! In fact young adults who choose to be active in the church are even more likely than older adults to be interested in Bible study, prayer, and spiritual growth.

7. Evaluate church programming. Is your church really focused on activities that "make a difference" in the lives of members and in society?

Or is your church caught in the trap of simply planning events and greasing the institutional wheels? Appeal to the desire of young adults to make a difference in individual lives, the church, and society.

8. Use both women and men in leadership positions. It isn't healthy for the majority of leadership positions in any church to be filled primarily by women or primarily by men. Young men are especially attracted to churches where men are involved in leadership positions. Likewise women want to see women in leadership roles.

9. Provide child care for worship services, classes, groups, and organizational meetings. No church will get heavy involvement from young adults with small children unless child care is available. Don't make the mistake of assuming that people will ask for it if they need it. Most young adults aren't comfortable saying that they can't be part of a particular activity because they can't arrange or can't afford a baby sitter. The church should always take the initiative in providing the service.

10. Create ways to use the talents of college and trade school students and other transient young adults in your community. While it is true that these young adults may only be in your community for a short period of time, it is still important to involve them—both because of the strength they will bring your church and because of the need for the church to reach out to them. If you have a college or trade school in your community, consider providing transportation to and from church worship services and other activities. Involve these people in leadership positions in the church by placing them on committees or in team teaching situations. Invite them to be ushers and choir members. Encourage them to help with task forces doing special events for the church or service projects for the community. Many churches miss large pools of young adult talent by not tak-

ing seriously the contributions that these groups can make.

11. Have a nominating committee that functions on a year-round basis rather than just at particular times. While it is true that most churches elect people to office at a specific time of the year (generally in the fall), potential leaders emerge throughout the year. The nominating committee should work cooperatively with the minister and other church leaders to identify young adults. Invite those young adults to share in leadership training. When they are enthusiastic and ready to go, involve them immediately in leadership positions.

12. When recruiting young adults (or anyone else, for that matter), the best responses always come from personal conversations rather than letters or phone calls. Take the time to sit down with the person being asked to assume a responsibility in the church. Explain the position fully, give the person a copy of the job description, share the tenure expectation, reinforce the reasons why you are inviting that person to accept the position, and answer questions.

Many churches find that using pairs of recruiters is the best approach. The presence of two people reinforces the importance of the position and the belief that the person being asked to assume the position is the right choice. Whenever possible, one member of the pair should be a young adult when a young adult is being recruited.

13. Use surveys and talent banks to identify the interests of young adults and others in the congregation. Many churches have developed the practice of having all members complete a form indicating their interest in helping in various areas and the skills that they have. Some medium-sized and large churches have found it useful to maintain that information on computer, which makes it very easy to find people with particular skills and interests. New members should

complete an information form during new member orientation.

14. Set up a special leadership team to improve the involvement of young adults in your church. That team should include a couple of members of the nominating committee and some young adults. The team can identify leaders and develop strategies for involving them. For more ideas, see the chapters on "Regaining Inactives" and "Reaching New Young Adults."

No one church is likely to implement every strategy described in this chapter, but you should be able to implement several of the preceding ideas. As your nominating committee or special young adult leadership committee discusses the 14 concepts presented in this chapter, those people will also identify other strategies that may be even better for your situation.

If your congregation is very small and the number of potential young adults even smaller, be sure that you involve those young adults in the top decision-making group of your church — the official board, board of deacons, trustees, or other group that makes the major decisions. If you can't involve young adults at every level, be sure you involve them where final decisions will be made!

Regaining Inactives

Steve Clapp

Sally has been a member of St. Matthew's since she was a child, and her parents are still active there. She's 29 years old, single (as the result of a divorce), a strong believer in Christ, but no longer active in the church.

She was involved in the church's youth group during her senior high years, and she always attended church while at home on vacation during her college years. Her wedding ceremony was held in St. Matthew's seven years ago, and she and her former husband attended worship services for two years after the wedding.

As the marriage started to sour, she and her husband got out of the habit of attending church. When the divorce came, her husband dropped out of the church completely. Sally has continued her membership but now limits her activity to attending the Christmas Eve communion service with her parents.

After her failed marriage, Sally isn't sure that she ever wants to get married again. She has, however, had a couple of serious relationships with the opposite sex since her marriage. She currently lives

with a man but has no intention of marrying him. When her minister visited, she spoke frankly about her lifestyle. She said that she just couldn't see that the church members she knew were able to accept her sexual relationship with a man outside of marriage. She is a forthright person and doesn't want to lie about it, but she also doesn't want to deal with rejection. She believes as strongly in God as ever and says that she would return to church if she ever decided to marry again and have children, but she's not expecting that to happen. She's immersed in her career and likes her present lifestyle.

It will not be easy for St. Matthew's to convince Sally to become active in the church again. Like most people, she's afraid of rejection; and she doesn't feel a strong need for the church at this point in her life.

Many circumstances have combined to cause a large number of young adults to be only nominal members of local churches. Reaching Sally and others like her is an important task, but it is also a very difficult task. Many churches have found that it's easier to reach new young adults than to reactivate those who are on the church rolls but no longer attend. The magnitude of the task, however, should not deter us from doing our best. People like Sally, if involved in the church again, bring great strength and energy.

It's tempting to think of people like Sally as the prodigal sons and daughters of the church, hoping to call them home. "For this son [or daughter] of mine was dead and is alive again; he [or she] was lost and is found!" (Luke 15:24). While the prodigal image may be accurate in many instances, it probably isn't the most helpful one for framing our approach to inactive young adults. For the most part, they don't think of themselves as prodigals, most do not want to be hit over the head with that image.

Why have so many young adults become inactive in the church? It's important to understand that loss of faith is not usually the reason young adults become inactive. The Wesley Kolbe survey referred to in "Young Adults in the '90s" found that there was no significant difference in the religious faith of those young adults who remain active in the church and those young adults who become inactive. They are just as likely to believe in God, to describe themselves as "born again," to believe in the power of prayer, and to believe in life after death.

Although there are significant exceptions, most young adults become inactive for one or two primary reasons:

1. They have lost the habit of regular attendance during their high school or early young adult years. They haven't returned either because they don't miss that involvement enough to be drawn by their own desire or because they feel uncomfortable returning after such along absence.

2. Something has happened within their own lives or the life of the church to disillusion them with the church as an organization — either the church in general or their particular congregation. This may take the form of deep seated anger or disappointment, but is just as likely to be a general feeling that religious needs and social needs are more readily met outside of the church.

In order to make a major effort at involving these young adults again, the first task you face is that of finding them. You want to identify both young adults who are formal members of your church and also young adults who may not be formal members but who at one time identified strongly with your congregation. You'll want to search:

- Church membership rolls for those young adults who belong but are no longer active.
- Church baptismal and confirmation rolls for those who at one time were a part of your church community but are not retained as active adult members. Many will have moved to other communities or actually joined other

churches. You need to go through those names, however, to be sure you haven't overlooked someone.

In a denomination that makes a distinction between baptism and confirmation, children and young people who are baptized sometimes fail to become confirmed as adult members. Those people, however, may still identify with your church and may even consider themselves members.

- Sunday school, youth group, and [C.C.D.] records from years back if those are available.
- Wedding records.
- Names from teachers and other leaders.

Consider as inactive members not only those who formally belong to your church (and don't attend) but also those who may consider themselves part of your church constituency because they have no other church affiliation. While that latter group may in some ways be viewed as "new" young adults and be reached by the strategies listed in the following chapter ("Reaching New Young Adults"), the strength of their earlier connection will make some of them respond as "inactive" young adults.

There are many approaches that you can take in efforts to reach these inactive young adults, but the most effective approaches always begin with face-to-face discussions with these people in their homes. There is simply no other equally effective way to find out why they are not involved and to reaffirm the church's interest in them. These young adults may have valuable program suggestions to share with you and feedback that will help you improve your church's young adult ministry.

Visits to these young adults should be made by a group of people who have discussed the visits in advance and have shared whatever they already know about the young adults who will be seen. If possible, go out in pairs with one member of each pair being a young adult who is active in the church. If that is not possible, forge ahead anyway!

It is very important to avoid dumping guilt on the inactive young adults for their failure to be involved; that is always a counterproductive strategy and can do great harm. Visitors should take the perspective that they are attempting to improve the church's ministry to young adults and want to visit with young adults to gain their perspectives and ideas. In that process, the church's interest in them can be strongly affirmed, and by the conclusion of the visit it should be natural to invite them to become involved again.

Some churches find it useful to conduct a survey of their young adult members. The survey can be completed during the process of visits in homes or can be conducted by telephone. It should not simply be mailed out, since doing that does very little to affirm the church's interest in these people and generally very few will mail the forms back. The survey information will be most useful if both active and inactive young adults are contacted. It is possible to contact active young adults through church school classes, social groups, or other program settings in the church.

The survey design which follows assumes that the survey will be conducted in an interview format either in person or over the telephone.

St. Matthew's Young Adult Survey

Name:_____
               (Include maiden name if applicable)
Age:_____Sex:_____
Marital status:_____

Names and ages of children if applicable:___
_____
_____

Church leadership positions presently held if
applicable: _____
_____
_____

Church classes or groups currently attended
if applicable:_____
_____
_____

Feelings about St. Matthew's Church
(Attempt to obtain an "open-ended" response.
If that isn't possible, then ask for an expres-
sion of feelings, with categories like: very
satisfied with St. Matthew's; somewhat satisfied; or not satisfied. Then attempt to obtain
reasons for the response. Don't be "pushy"
but make it clear that the response is important.):
_____
_____
_____
_____
_____
_____

Interested in a short term (6-8 week) Bible study group?
                    ____ Yes____ No

Interested in a weekly Christian education class for young adults?
                    ____ Yes____ No

Interested in a monthly social group for young adults?
                    ____ Yes____ No

Interested in the choir?
                    ____ Yes____ No

Interested in being an usher?
                    ____ Yes____ No

Interested in being on a board or committee?
                    ____ Yes____ No

If yes, which one? _____

What suggestions do you have for the improvement of St. Matthew's programs for young adults?
_____
_____
_____
_____
_____

What suggestions do you have for the overall improvement of St. Matthew's?
_____
_____
_____
_____
_____

You may wish to give the task of visiting young adults and obtaining survey information to the young adult leadership team described in suggestion 14 of the chapter "Young Adults in Church Leadership." Information obtained in the survey will also be helpful in designing programs and strategies for reaching new young adults who have not been previously connected with your church.

In the process of following up on young adults who have become inactive, you will find some who have moved out of the community. You probably will not be able to visit with those individuals in person, but attempt phone calls where possible. Use the contact to find out if they anticipate moving back to your community at some future time; this will often be the case for college students and military personnel. In those instances, you want to be sure that these people receive the church newsletter or some other periodic communication from the church.

If these people do not anticipate returning to your community, then you want to encourage them to join a church in the new community. You may wish to make contact with a church of your own denomination in that community and urge the new church to invite the young adult(s) to services and activities.

Resist the temptation to simply "clean up the church rolls" by dropping these members. Do all you can to see that they become involved in another congregation. College students and military personnel should be encouraged to be involved in a congregation in their community of temporary residence even if your church will remain their "church home." Many denominations have programs of "associate membership" for people in such situations.

You will probably also find a few people who are still in your community and have actually joined other churches but never bothered to have themselves removed from your membership rolls.

In such instances, you of course want to remove their names but be sure that you communicate that you are pleased they have found a church home that is comfortable for them. You also want to discover, if possible, why they chose to join another church; that information may help you evaluate your own church.

Do not feel threatened by the fact that they are more comfortable in another congregation. Remember that the overall goal should be to help people draw closer to Christ and live in meaningful ways. If someone can do that more comfortably in another church, then that is cause for rejoicing rather than bitterness or sadness. No congregation can meet the needs of every single person, and we are all part of the body of Christ.

Reaching New Young Adults

Steve Clapp

Jim is 28 years old, single, a loan officer at a bank, and not a church member. A cashier at the bank discovered during a coffee break conversation that Jim has a strong interest in the Bible. She invited him to share in a small Bible study group that meets in her neighborhood each Thursday evening. The participants take turns hosting the group in their homes. He was a little uneasy about accepting the invitation because the study group is sponsored by her church, and he said that he wasn't comfortable about church membership. She reassured him that there was no pressure to join the church and that people in the group were very open.

Jim started attending the group and found himself looking forward to it each week. Jim began to recognize that this group filled a major void in his life. He found himself opening some of his deepest feelings to the group and felt he had truly been blessed when other group members shared some of their deepest thoughts. He had always believed in Christ, but he had never felt Christ's presence as strongly as in this group of people. He met the church's minister at one of the sessions, and two months later started attending worship services. Two months after that, Jim joined the church.

Annie and Mark are in their early thirties, have busy jobs, have no children, and have no church home. The plight of the homeless has been of deep concern to them, partly because Annie remembers stories of her uncle, who was homeless for two years and froze to death in a severe Michigan winter. They consider themselves religious people but have had no particular interest in the church.

A friend of Annie's asked if they would consider helping with the emergency winter shelter program at the church. Volunteers were continually needed to prepare meals and supervise the homeless people who gathered in the church basement to sleep on cots. Annie and Mark gladly shared with Annie's friend and two other people in working at the shelter one night a week.

As they talked more with church members, they felt themselves drawing closer to them and beginning to appreciate what the church at its best could mean. The companionship they shared with the other shelter volunteers was the most enjoyable and meaningful they'd had since college. They also found themselves growing closer to the homeless people, some of whom were beginning to attend the church. Nine months later they joined the church.

Susan has a beautiful voice and had life gone a little differently, she might have become a professional musician. She's in her early twenties, single, and not a church member. A neighbor heard Susan singing through an open apartment window and later made an appreciative comment to her. The neighbor is active in her local church and greatly enjoys the choir. She invited Susan to join the choir, assuring her that there would be no pressure about church membership.

At first Susan didn't accept the invitation. She recognized that her neighbor was sincere about not putting pressure on her, but she had a feeling that the church's minister and some of the other choir members would not be so considerate. Her neighbor's gentle persistence paid off, however, and Susan, feeling lonely much of the time, decided that the choir might be worth a try. She found herself drawn into the warmth of the choir and the church, made a new commitment to Christ, and joined the congregation.

Carol and Eddie are in their late twenties and have just had their first child. A neighbor of theirs is a widow in her sixties, and she quickly became a foster grandparent to the new child. The neighbor asked Carol and Eddie how they felt about baptism of the child and about the possibility of the child having contact with the church.

Carol and Eddie both consider themselves religious people but without a need for the formal structure of a church. As they visited with their neighbor, however, they began to see that the community of the church could mean a great deal to a developing child. They started attending worship services and a Bible study group, had the child baptized, and joined the church. Now the congregation has become the center of their social life, and they are both thoroughly involved in all kinds of church activities.

The examples just shared are reasonably typical ones, and some important observations can be made:

1. In each instance, a person *invited* the young adult(s) into some kind of church involvement. Most people get involved in a church because a person they know asks them to become involved. Any strategy for involving young adults that fails to recognize this basic reality is not likely to succeed.

2. In three of the four instances, the initial invitation that was accepted was not to worship services or church membership but to involve-

ment in a group within the church. The group life of the church provides many ports of entry that are very important.

3. Warm invitations were extended in each instance, but those offering the invitations and others involved in the church were careful not to put pressure on the young adults. The young adults were permitted to choose their own levels of involvement and made to feel welcome and accepted.

4. The desire for intimacy, to be close to God and to other people, creates an openness to group involvement. When that desire is met by group involvement, people find themselves wanting to join the church.

5. The birth of a first child is always a very significant time at which far more people than usual are open to the possibility of church membership.

Previous chapters in this book, especially "Young Adults in the '90s," have helped explain the importance of intimacy to young adults and have identified some of the characteristics of young adults who are not members of churches. It is especially important to remember:

- That the majority of those who are not church members nevertheless do believe in God and will react negatively to the implication that their faith is inadequate or not complete. They may respond positively to opportunities to deepen that faith, provided the opportunities are offered without the implication that the nonmembers are in some way inferior.

- That those not in church, like those heavily involved in the church, have a deep-seated need for intimacy both with God and with others. Opportunities to meet that need will have a positive response.

- Young adults who are not involved in the church may feel differently than church-involved adults about several things. For example, they are more likely to think there is nothing wrong with moderate consumption of alcohol, that premarital intercourse is all right when there is some degree of caring between the two people, that discrimination in hiring and pay should be eliminated, and that personal faith can be validly expressed without being part of a church. Initial tolerance of those attitudes on the part of church members is an important part of reaching and involving these young adults.

Finding Young Adults

1. As shown by the examples with which this chapter opened, your present church members are the people most likely to meaningfully reach young adults. Help church members be sensitive to young adults they meet in their neighborhoods, community organizations, and at work. Work through classes, groups, choirs, organizations, boards, and committees of your church to help motivate members to reach out to others.

2. Make contact with people in your community who are likely to come into contact with many young adults. Those people may have valuable information to share with you. Consult college administrators, foremen at factories, workers in utility companies, real estate agents, apartment complex managers, bankers, employment agency directors, and "welcome wagon" type organizations. Find out what the needs of young adults are, and develop programs to meet those needs.

3. Consider doing a house-to-house survey to locate young adults and other potential members in neighborhoods served by your church or in neighborhoods that *should* be served by your church. Have volunteers go house to house to find out if people have a church home. When people do have a church home, thank them for the information and go to the next address. When people do not, have a brochure about your

church to leave and ask for the answers to some
questions about the household (approximate ages,
marital status, children, employment, interest in
the church, interest in the choir, interest in study
or fellowship groups, etc.).

Develop Programs to Meet the Needs of Young Adults

As you gain more contact with young adults in
your community and learn more about their
needs, develop programs in response to those
needs. For example:
- Offer weekend spiritual life retreats.
- Have short-term or long-term relational Bible
  study groups (using resources such as the
  Covenant Bible Study Series available from
  faithQuest).
- Start a monthly social group for young adult
  couples.
- Start a breakfast Bible study group.
- Have a weekly movie and pizza group.
- Start a social group for young singles (with
  hors d'oeuvres and drinks).
- Have a seminar on parenting for new parents.
- Begin a support group for people who have
  recently been divorced or are trying to hold a
  marriage together.
- Begin a support group for people who have
  had problems with an addiction (alcohol, to-
  bacco, or other drugs).
- Offer a marriage enrichment retreat twice a
  year.
- Have a seminar on "Finding New Jobs" and
  promote it in the community.
- Start a Toastmasters Club for your neighborhood with meetings held at the church. These
  clubs provide significant help for people who
  want to gain skill at self-expression that will
  help them move ahead professionally.

- Have a "Money Management Seminar" and promote it in the community.
- Start a support group for single parents.
- Start a service program such as a food pantry or emergency shelter and seek young adult help in that program's operation.

Child Care, Day Care, and Nursery School

As mentioned in the chapter on "Young Adults in Church Leadership," it's crucial for your church to provide child care at all church activities if you want to gain the involvement of young adults who have children. That needs to be part of the planning process for all groups, classes, organizations, and meetings that hope to involve young adults with children.

Some churches have day care and nursery school programs through the week. Far more churches do not sponsor such programs themselves but permit the use of their facilities by day care centers and nursery schools. More stringent regulations on day care centers and nursery schools have made some churches more reluctant to have or host these activities, but the need for these services is enormous—and almost all the adults who use these services for their children are young adults! Quality day care or nursery schools in your church can do a great deal to draw young adults to your church and is a significant service to the community.

If you have a day care or nursery school, be sure that those using the service have the opportunity to get acquainted with some church members and with your minister. You don't want to be "pushy," but you do want to share genuine interest in these people.

What Is It Like to Visit Your Church?

Take a critical look at your church. As you seek to draw more young adults and other potential members, be sure that there are no major "turn-offs" for those who come. How would you answer the following questions if you were coming to your church for the first time?

1. How easy is it to locate the church?

2. How does the outside of the church look? Does it look like people care about the church?

3. How easy is it to find a parking place? If parking is available in the lots of neighboring businesses, is that clearly indicated?

4. Can visitors tell which entrance to use for the sanctuary? for the church school? for the minister's office?

5. Are there designated greeters who can see that people get to the right places for worship, education, and child care?

6. Is the order of worship easy to follow for a visitor?

7. Are visitors normally greeted before and after worship services, or can they sneak in and sneak out? Is the way in which visitors are recognized comfortable, or does it make visitors feel awkward?

8. Is there a registration process for visitors, so that the church can follow up later? Is that process clear and easy to understand?

9. Is there a coffee and cookie time or other informal opportunity for people to socialize? If so, are visitors made to feel welcome during this time or left to stand awkwardly alone?

10. Is child care provided? Do the people who staff the child care communicate warmth to the children and their parents? Would you feel comfortable leaving your children in the child care program of the church?

What happens after people visit your congregation is also extremely important:

11. Does your church rely only on a letter for contact with those who visit worship services? Growing churches have learned that personal visits by lay volunteers and staff are the best way to turn visitors into members. The visits should not be "pushy" but should be warm and supportive. When possible, have other young adults call on the young adults who visit your worship services.

12. Are the names of young adults who visit worship services passed on to classes, groups, and the choir? Positive contacts can be made by these organizations.

13. Does a young adult leadership team, the church staff, or another group in the church do continued follow up with those who visit worship services or a group in the church?

14. If people who visit your church indicate that they are members of another congregation, of course you should respect that situation and thank them for having come. If they are not members of another church and express clearly that they do not wish to become members of your church, do you do your best to understand why they feel that way? There may be things you can learn from their rejection or lack of interest that will help your church more effectively reach others.

15. Have people in your choir, classes, groups, and organizations been helped to understand the importance of sharing warmth and openness but avoiding "pushiness" with potential members? The right attitude from these people can do a great deal to help your church.

Singles in a Family World

Steve Clapp

Strong family programs are an important part of virtually every church, and no one would want to neglect an emphasis on the family in order to reach singles. It is important, however, for churches to reflect a broader emphasis on the family of God, which includes all people regardless of marital status.

The average age for a person's first marriage has continued to rise with the result that more people stay single for longer periods of time. Some people choose an intentional single lifestyle with no plans for marriage.

Young singles are not the only ones who may feel shut out of the life of the church. As average life expectancy increases in the United States, large numbers of church members outlive their spouses and become older singles. While many of them will marry again, many will not. The divorce rate also creates larger numbers of singles than in some past generations.

Here are some statements that young adult singles made in one study about their involvement with the church (Wesley Kolbe, 1988):

- "The way the minister speaks on Sunday morning makes me feel like being single just isn't as good as being married. It's like you aren't quite a full member of the Christian community. I don't think he really means it like that, but that's how it makes me feel."
- "I've tried attending a Sunday school class several times, but it never quite works for me. Almost everyone else is married and I don't feel comfortable with some of the conversations."
- "My church talks about wanting to do something to reach young singles, but they seem reluctant to initiate any new programming. They have groups and classes for families and then just kind of say 'Well, singles are welcome too.' I think they'd have better results if they tried a group that was just for singles."
- "Staying in my church after my divorce was a real struggle. Part of it was just that people felt awkward. They were used to my being present with my husband, and then he wasn't there any longer. And there was this feeling that I picked up that if I had been the right kind of person, then I wouldn't have had a divorce. But those people don't know what I was going through. I've never in my life needed understanding and compassion as much as I did with the divorce, and the church really failed me. I still attend worship because I feel like I owe that to God, but I don't feel the same way about the people in the church."
- "I've always been active in the church, but I feel dishonest some of the time. I'm not married, and I'm not at all sure that I'm going to get married. That doesn't mean I have a celibate lifestyle. I don't sleep around with just anyone. I feel like that's wrong, and it's also

stupid. There has to be some commitment before I'll sleep with someone. I can't talk about that in any group in the church though. People just can't deal with the fact that I'm a single person and sexually active."

Statements from the pulpit, in the church newsletter, and in church organizations need to make it clear that all people are part of the church family. Jesus was single. As far as we are aware, the apostle Paul was single. Surely those and other biblical examples provide a strong case for the legitimacy of a single lifestyle.

The church needs to recognize the need of all people to be part of a caring, intimate community. The church should offer those kinds of opportunities for people of all ages, whether single or married. When relating to people who have been divorced or who are single parents, the attitude of the Christian community should always be one of acceptance and caring.

The remainder of this chapter is devoted to some specific suggestions for improving your church's outreach to single young adults. You may also wish to look carefully at the ideas in "Starting New Groups" and "Reaching New Young Adults."

1. Be sure that you have single young adults as part of decision-making groups in the church. This is the best way to be certain that their needs are met and that their perspective is recognized. It's especially important to have single young adults on the top decision-making body in your church.

2. Ministers should carefully review their sermons and prayers to be certain that single young adults (and older singles as well) will not feel excluded or perhaps even offended by what is said. The minister should also be an advocate of the needs of singles as he or she works with the various groups and organizations in the church.

3. If there is a trade school or college in your community, see what kind of outreach your

church may develop to young adults who are attending classes. You may find that a special
study or social group is needed. You may also
wish to help with transportation from a school
campus to your church for worship services and
other activities.

4. Consider developing a mentoring program
for the singles in your congregation. This is especially valuable for young people who have recently
graduated from high school. An older member of
the church is assigned as a "mentor" to a young
single. The relationship should not be one of parenting but one of friendship. The older adult can
share encouragement with the young single in
terms of faith development, career goals, and life
decisions. Meeting together once a month for
breakfast, lunch, or supper is an ideal way to
maintain the relationship. Both the young adult
and the older member will grow as a result of
their time together.

5. Use Bible study groups to involve young
singles. If your church is sufficiently large or
there are large numbers of young adults in the
community, you may wish to have one or more
Bible study groups just for singles. If that isn't
realistic, then give careful consideration to how
singles may be involved and helped to feel accepted in groups that include people who are
married. Many young singles have a deep thirst
for knowledge of the Bible and want help in growing closer to God. They will very often respond
positively when invited to participate in a Bible
study group.

6. Form a social group for young singles. This
can be an excellent port of entry for young singles in the community who are not part of any
church. Successful social groups often include the
sharing of an informal meal, which is an excellent
way to build relationships and work toward the
kind of intimacy that people seek in the Christian
community.

7. Form a support group for single parents. This may be initially focused on single parents in your church, but it can also be a significant form of outreach to the community. Large numbers of single parents are in strong need of the kind of caring and encouragement that the church at its best can offer. You may reach some singles who are a few years out of the young adult range, but the common bond of being single parents will pull group members together.

8. Consider the possibility of a support group for people who are going through a divorce or who have recently been divorced. Depending on the size of your community, you may reach large numbers of young adults in this way. While the church obviously wants to help preserve marriage, it is always appropriate to extend care to those going through the pain of divorce. A support group can be a good port of entry to your church for new members, and the group will be deeply appreciated by those already in your church. As with the group for single parents, you will reach some people who are past the young adult range, but the common bonds will hold the group together.

9. Hold seminars on specific themes of interest to young singles in your church and community. Some possibilities:

- Seminars on self-esteem are of value to virtually all young singles.
- Seminars on vocational choice may be of special value to those in the early young adult years.
- Seminars on sexuality can be of great help to young adults in the difficult decisions that they face in this area. Be sure the tone is nonjudgmental and supportive, so that people are free to express their feelings and grapple with the teachings of the church.

10. Hold a spiritual life retreat for young singles. Vast numbers of young singles are interested in developing the spiritual life. A weekend of Bible

study, prayer, and discussion can deepen their faith and help them build deeper relationships with one another. Young adults in the community who are uneasy about joining the church may nevertheless be willing to make a commitment to a weekend experience.

The most creative church programming possible will not be effective unless people are invited to participate. As you begin new groups or work to integrate young singles into existing groups, be sure that invitations for involvement are shared on a personal level. You'll find further suggestions for reaching people in "Starting New Groups" and "Reaching New Young Adults."

The Changing Nature of Marriage and Family

Don Booz

The institution of marriage and the family is in a constant state of formation, maintenance, or dissolution. Anxiety and perhaps fear that the traditional American family may be breaking down or even going out of existence is expressed by many in the church today. Some of the fear stems from the increasing number of single-parent families and the number of divorces. Others point to drug abuse, sexual promiscuity, and declining morality as major factors in the breakdown of the family. People worry that the rising divorce rate, the falling birth rate, and the increasing number of working mothers will force the family into extinction.

Given all of the data available, it is safe to say that marriages and families are in a period of transition and redefinition. Exactly how today's young adults will change the definition, purpose, and function of marriages and families remains to be seen.

Parents once thought that when their children turned 18, their parental duties were done and they could send the children off to school, to work, or to marry. Today we live in a different world. As one parent who recently allowed an adult child to return home to live said, "I'm not sure that young adults know how to leave home. Maybe that is the place where we, as parents, have failed the most. I always worried about drugs and premarital sex and it never occurred to me that we would have a 26-year-old child living with us."

Leaving home has become more complex and living arrangements are more varied among young adults today. Leaving home in contemporary America follows three basic patterns. In one the maturing child remains at home until completing school and then almost immediately leaves home fully financially independent. In a second pattern, the maturing child leaves home to continue his or her education. Consequently, the higher education institution becomes a surrogate parent to the young adult. The third pattern is when, after school ends, the child makes no residential change. Subsequently, the child remains at home while often contributing financially to the parental household (Goldscheider 111).

In 1989, 13.4 million adults ages 18 to 24 and 4.9 million ages 25 to 34 lived in the homes of their parents. Virtually all (97 percent) of the men and women in this age group who lived with their parents had never been married. Although men were more likely than women to live with their parents, women were more likely than men to ever have been married (U.S. Bureau of the Census, Current Population Reports, Series P-20, No. 445). One 28-year-old man who described his living at home as a financial necessity, said, "I'm not sure if I will ever get married because I am living exactly the way I would want to live away from home."

Leaving home seems to be related to several factors. The most consistent influence is the cost of rental housing and the income levels of the young adult. Some have observed that higher incomes and a higher housing availability in a given area have a strong influence on both leaving home and living with roommates (Christian 66). Another factor in leaving home is living in an area with higher educational levels. A reason for young adults to continue to live at home may be that a large number of them are continuing their education and it is more convenient to live at home (Riche 125).

For many young adults, leaving home may take time to happen. They eventually do leave home but perhaps not in the way the parent(s) may want it to happen (Haines 151). The Census Bureau's current Population Report of March 1989 indicates that the number of unmarried-couple households in 1989 was approximately 2.8 million up from 523,000 in 1970.

More and more young adults are opting for a lifestyle that moves toward "close relationships" and "strong friendships" as possible partnerships with another person. Furthermore, "community" and "weekend experiences" are becoming more prevalent as an alternative structure for intimacy needs of the young adult. As one person recently told me, "I save up my money all year long in order to go to Club Med." As a pastor, the most common question I hear is "Where do I go to meet people my age?" More frequently, people are living together but keeping separate checking accounts while sharing the costs of maintaining household expenses.

Many changes have occurred in the living arrangements and the marital status of young adults over the past several decades. These changes include a trend toward postponement of first marriages, a growing proportion of never-married people, and adults who reside in unmarried-couple households.

By definition, unrelated adults living together in a sexual relationship is called cohabitation. One explanation for the increase in cohabitation is a relaxation of societal attitudes toward sexual behavior. Marriage is no longer reserved for the "first time" experience for sexual partners. Consequently, extended periods of cohabitation have diminished the need for formalized marriage (Spanier 101). However, current population statistics are not needed to observe that young adults are either cohabitating or choosing to marry at a later age.

In 1989, the estimated median age of first marriage was 26.2 years for men and 23.8 years for women. Between 1975 and 1989 the median age has risen 2.7 years for both men and women after increasing by only 1 year during the 20 years spanning 1955 to 1975. The proportion of both men and women in their 20s and early 30s who have never married has grown substantially during the past two decades. Between 1970 and 1989, the proportion never married at age 20 to 24 increased by 75 percent for women and 41 percent for men (U.S. Bureau of the Census, Current Population Reports, Series P-20, No. 445).

Although Current Population Surveys indicate that married-couple families remain the most common type of living arrangement, the proportion of households accounted for by two-parent families has dramatically declined. While married-couple families without children present accounted for almost as high a proportion of households in 1990 as they did 20 years ago, the proportion of households accounted for by two-parent families (married-couple families with one or more children under 18) has declined dramatically. Only 26 percent of households were two-parent families in 1990, down from 31 percent in 1980 and 40 percent in 1970. Thus, there has been a decline of about 14 percentage points since 1970 in the share of households that are composed of two-parent families. Single-parent situations and families maintained by women have increased from 17 percent to 25 percent of all households between 1970 and 1990. Another trend over the last 20 years is fewer children per family and/or postponement of parenthood (National Center for Health Statistics).

The review of the literature attributes several reasons for the postponement of parenthood. Couples are marrying later and the availability of contraceptives helps postpone parenthood. It is quite evident from the research that delayed childbearing is more common in dual-career marriages. This has been attributed to couples having babies on their own terms, both economically and emotionally. Having a child later in life is seen as having the advantages for the parents of increased maturity and financial security, and a greater chance of the parents achieving personal career goals. Indications are that this trend will continue and more couples will opt for postponing parenthood (Schlesinger 355-363, Wineberg 99-110).

Equality between the sexes and differing expectations from marriage continue to be a source of tension. More and more women are entering the work force and many families are not like the Huxtables on "The Cosby Show." The division of labor tends to fall along traditional lines with a lack or even an absence of equality in sharing household tasks. Despite a growing number of women who believe that men should share in household responsibilities, men still see themselves as the "head of the household" (Mintz 111). However, women who work are increasing their impact and power in the decision-making process of the family despite the inequality in the housework (Miller 237-296). It remains to be seen exactly how these changes will affect the family in the future.

Implications for the Church

What we are seeing today in our churches is not so much a breakdown of the family but, rather, the emergence of different patterns and a redefinition of marriage and family life. In today's society, young adults have more choices of life-style than ever before. Not only are young adults leaving home later, they are tending to postpone marriage and childbearing. Furthermore, cohabitation, as an alternative form to marriage, is most likely to continue. This shift in life patterns will undoubtedly cause the church to re-think its ministry with the young adult.

Questions the church will need to answer in the future are: How will the church define families without excluding the young adult? What form of ministry will include the diversity of needs and the various lifestyles of the young adult? How will the denominations that practice infant baptism and child dedication accept parents living together but not married? In what ways can the church accept singleness as an intentional lifestyle?

The evidence shows that today's young adults will continue to organize their relationships in varied ways. The church will need to re-think who sits in the family pew on Sunday mornings. In order to address the needs of young adults, the first thing the church will need to do is get to know them. The second thing to accomplish is involvement of young adults in church planning sessions. And the third achievement is to organize the church program in such a way that new ideas and changes can occur. But the most important advance will be the development of a more open and accepting attitude toward young adults.

We do not know how the next generation of young adults will experience the need for even the idea of marriage and the family. We do know that young adults need and want to participate in the life of the church. To provide a place in the community of believers for young adults is the most important ministry the church can provide.

References

Christian, Patricia. "Nonfamily Households and Housing Among Young Adults" in *Ethnicity and the New Family Economy*, eds. Francis K. Goldscheider and Calvin Goldscheider. San Francisco: Westview Press, 1989.

Goldscheider, Francis. "Children Leaving Home and the Household Economy" in *Ethnicity and the New Family Economy*, eds. Francis K. Goldscheider and Calvin Goldscheider. San Francisco: Westview Press, 1989.

Haines, James and Neely, Margery. *Parents' Work Is Never Done*. Far Hills: New Horizon Press, 1989.

Miller, J. and Garrison, H. "Sex Roles: The Division of Labor at Home and in the Workplace." *Annual Review of Sociology*, 8, 1982, pp. 237-296.

Mintz, Steven and Kellogg, Susan. "Coming Apart: Radical Departures Since 1990" in *Marriage and Family in Transition*, eds. John Edwards and David Demo. Boston: Allyn and Bacon, 1991.

National Center for Health Statistics. *Advance report of final marriage statistics, 1987*. Monthly vital statistics report, vol. 38, no. 12, suppl. Public Health Service: Hyattsville, Maryland, 1990.

Riche, Martha. "Mysterious Young Adults" in *Family in Transition*, eds. Arlene Skolnick and Jerome Skolnick, . Boston: Scott, Foresman and Company, 1989.

Schlesinger, B. and Schlesinger, R. "Postponed Parenthood: Trends and Issues." *Journal of Comparative Family Studies*, 20, Autumn, 1989, pp. 355-363.

Spanier, Graham. "Cohabitation: Recent Changes in the United States" in *Marriage and Family in Transition*, eds. John Edwards and David Demo. Boston: Allyn and Bacon, 1991.

U.S. Bureau of the Census, Current Population Reports, Series P-20, No. 445, Marital Status and Living Arrangements: March 1989, U.S. Government Printing Office, Washington, DC, 1990.

U.S. Bureau of the Census, Current Population Reports, Series P-20, No. 447, Household and Family Characteristics: March 1990 and 1989, U.S. Government Printing Office, Washington, DC, 1990.

Wineberg, Howard. "Delayed Childbearing, Childlessness and Marital Disruption" in *Journal of Comparative Family Studies*, 21, Spring, 1990, pp. 99-100.

Starting New Groups

Steve Clapp

Oak Lawn Church has 500 adult members. Not nearly as many are young adults as should be, based on the neighborhoods served by the Oak Lawn Church. A special task force on young adult ministry decides to initiate the following new groups over a fifteen-month period of time:

- Two neighborhood Bible study groups to serve apartment complexes with high numbers of young adults. The core group to start each Bible study has already been identified.
- A supper club for young singles, to meet on Sunday evenings. Group members will get together at the church and then cook a meal or go to a restaurant together. The group will occasionally have a speaker but will more often have open discussion during its time together. A core group has been identified and is enthusiastic about the idea. They plan on heavy publicity in the church and in the community.
- A seminar on parenting, which will meet on six consecutive Wednesday

evenings. This will be aimed at the parents of children in the church's day care center, and there will be other efforts to reach new parents in the community.

- A support group called "When Living Hurts," aimed at helping people who are depressed and those living with people who have significant problems with depression. This will not be limited by age, but the task force working on young adult ministry recognized that several young adults in the community have trouble dealing with depression. By designing the group not only for those who are ready to acknowledge their own problems with depression, but also for those who have friends or family members they want to help deal with depression, any stigma has been removed from participating in the group. A clinical psychologist will give help when needed, but the task force plans primarily on a common sense, self-help approach. They will use as a resource Sol Gordon's book *When Living Hurts*.

Obviously the Oak Lawn Church has planned an ambitious 15 months with that many new groups. Most churches will not want to undertake that much in a 15-month period of time. Note, however, the care that has been taken in the planning process:

- A task force has looked at young adult ministry needs and opportunities.
- A target audience has been determined for each of the groups. None are simply aimed at "all young adults."
- A core membership group has also been identified for each group, along with specific plans for reaching a larger number of people.
- The plan includes short-term as well as long-term opportunities.
- The task force doesn't plan to start all the new groups at the same time but to space them out over a 15-month period to permit

appropriate emphasis to be given to each strategy.

Your church may not be large enough for that many new groups in one year, but the kind of planning done by the Oak Lawn Church sets a good example. In general most churches find it easier to begin new groups for young adults than to increase the size of existing groups in the church. There are several reasons why new groups are often more successful:

- There are limitations on how large a given group is likely to become. Although Sunday school classes are occasionally 50 or more people in size, that is the exception rather than the rule. Most groups have a tendency to stop growing when they reach 15-25 in average attendance. A social group such as the supper club may be larger, but relational Bible study groups are most meaningful with 10-15 participants.
- There are always some barriers for new people joining a group that has been meeting for several months or years. No matter how accepting people in the group are, new members have some discomfort for their first few weeks of participation. Some people remain through that period of discomfort. Others do not.
- There is a sense of excitement in being part of a new group or venture. Many people like being in the core group that establishes something new, and others like joining in the enthusiasm.
- A new group, such as a supper club or a support group to help with depression, is newsworthy. Radio stations and newspapers are far more likely to give publicity to the formation of such a group than to events hosted by an existing group.

As you plan for new groups in your church, keep in mind the reality that short-term groups are sometimes less threatening to nonmembers or new members than continuing groups. A short-term group represents a well-defined commitment for a weekend, three sessions, six sessions, ten sessions, or whatever is determined. Some people who aren't sure about joining a class or group that meets every week on a continuing basis are much more willing to join a short-term group.

The group in your church looking at young adult ministries may want to brainstorm creative responses to the needs of young adults in the community. You may come up with a variety of creative group and class ideas. Then you can select the best idea or ideas for implementation. You may want to review some of the program suggestions in "Reaching New Young Adults" and other chapters. Groups or events like the following are often a part of successful young adult ministries. Remember, however, that a group will only be successful if it truly meets perceived needs of young adults in your church and community.

- Relational Bible study groups (using resources such as *faithQuest's* Covenant Bible Study Series).
- Social groups (meeting weekly, bimonthly, or monthly). Perhaps for all young adults; more often focused on singles or married couples.
- Supper clubs like the one described for the Oak Lawn Church.
- Support groups for people sharing a common need. Note the example of a "When Living Hurts" group given for the Oak Lawn Church. Groups for divorced people, single parents, and students can be an effective form of outreach.
- Breakfast Bible study groups meeting early in the morning for a light breakfast and Bible study. Some churches have established these at locations near where members work.
- "Mother's Afternoon Out" groups for young parents. Child care is provided at the church, and the mothers have the opportunity to share in discussion, study, or recreation.

They may sometimes elect to go shopping together.

- Marriage enrichment retreats. The Roman Catholic marriage encounter model is an excellent one.
- Spiritual life retreats. Use materials such as the Covenant Bible Study Series or other resources.
- Marriage enrichment seminars at the church.
- Spiritual life seminars.
- Movie clubs. These are especially popular with young singles. The group meets to attend a motion picture together or watch a video and then shares food and discussion. A number of popular motion pictures raise questions of significance for the Christian faith.
- Parenting seminars. Have a series of classes like those planned by the Oak Lawn Church for the benefit of young parents. Use a variety of resource people or good study materials. The content is best determined by a planning committee consisting of people who will participate in the seminar.
- Book clubs. Have a group that meets monthly, bimonthly, or weekly to talk abut books of interest to the group. A great many young adults read widely and welcome the opportunity to share reflections with one another.
- "Finding a Better Job" seminars. Use community resource people to plan a seminar to help young adults improve their vocational situation. This can be of interest to both single and married young adults across a fairly wide age range.
- "Choosing a Vocation" seminars for young adults just out of high school, to help them in vocational and educational choices.
- Groups that are centered on providing a needed service such as renovating homes for low-income families, providing emergency shelter during the winter, operating an emergency food pantry, or providing a daily or

weekly meal for those who are poor. While the makeup of these groups often includes people of a wide age span, they are especially attractive to many concerned young adults.

- Groups that are centered on a particular issue of importance to young adults and others in your area. Groups might focus on feminist issues, world peace, poverty, honest government, drug and alcohol problems, or other topics of concern.
- Summer vacation groups. Have a group get together to plan and take a summer trip. These activities are especially popular with young singles and can be done in ways that save money for all the participants. Some churches rent a summer house on Cape Cod, along the Great Lakes, in Corpus Christi, along the Florida coast, or in another popular location and then schedule it for young singles and/or young couples throughout the summer months.
- Seminars on self-confidence or building intimacy. Terry Hershey's book *Go Away Come Closer* is an excellent resource for a group wanting to better understand intimacy.

No matter what kind of group you start, there are some important steps to consider if you want the group to be a success. The following factors should be part of your planning process:

1. Define the group carefully:
- What is the target group of people you want to reach (singles, couples, people in a specific neighborhood, people in college, single parents, divorced people, etc.)?
- How long should the group continue? Is it short term or long term?
- What is the topic or purpose of the group?
- What are the minimum and maximum numbers for the group?
- Are you reasonably confident that a core group (two to six people) is interested or can be interested in the group?

2. Recruit between two and six people as a "core group" who will become the initial planning group and participate in the group once it begins meeting formally.

3. Be certain you have good leadership for the group. In some instances you may want to recruit the leader before the core group; in other instances you may want the core group to recruit the leader. Even if the group is itself a social group, which will elect its own officers once it begins meeting, you at least need a designated coordinator who will take initial responsibility.

In selecting leaders, you want to look for people who are themselves young adults or who can relate well to young adults, who have a healthy appreciation for diversity and aren't judgmental or domineering toward others, who have a strong commitment to helping the group be successful, and who have whatever content knowledge or skills are important for the particular kind of group. Sometimes an interested person can receive training or do personal study to pick up needed content knowledge. A person does not, for example, have to be a biblical scholar to give leadership to a relational Bible study group. Excellent materials are available to help such groups, and there should be strong member participation. What is essential for that kind of group is a willingness to study and to enable others to participate. On the other hand, the leader for the initial meetings of a group for divorced people should have some background and skill in support group work in order to get the group off to a good start.

4. Have the core group begin contacting other people who would gain from participation in such a group. Also have core group members check with the minister and other church members for the names of people who would enjoy the group. Rely primarily on person-to-person recruitment rather than printed announcements and other publicity as the group comes together. Printed announcements and other publicity can play an

important role, but most people who choose to participate can play an important role, but most people who choose to participate will do so because another person invites them.

5. Involve those with a commitment to the group in setting the day and time for the first meeting and for future meetings.

6. Use bulletins, worship service announcements, and the church newsletter for added publicity; but remember that steps two and four are your most important in membership recruitment. You may also consider publicity in the community through direct mail or phone calls to young adults who have been identified by your church; posters in area grocery stores, fitness centers, etc.; newspaper articles; and public service announcements on radio and television stations. The more service-oriented or support-oriented the group, the more likely that you can receive substantial help from the media. In announcements and news releases, be sure to indicate clearly where and when the group meets (or will begin to meet) and provide a telephone number for people wanting further information.

7. Include get-acquainted activities in the first several sessions. Share a meal together if possible. Group members need informal as well as formal time so that strong bonds are formed early in the life of the group. This is important whether the group is meeting for only four weeks, one weekend, or the next several years.

8. Unless your church is very large and has many good staff and volunteer resources, don't try to start more than one group at a time. Even a church as large as Oak Lawn decided to spread the start of the four new program groups over a 15-month period of time. Trying to do too much at once puts the groups in competition for publicity and participation.

9. Leave some decisions for the group itself to make once members begin meeting. The core group needs to have enough planned that the

group doesn't flounder, but others who come for the initial session need to have a sense of ownership. Will there be coffee and tea at group meetings? What will the next topic of study be? Will there be a group supper (assuming the group itself isn't a supper club)? What other resources should the group use?

10. Keep accurate attendance records and follow up quickly on any breaks in attendance. When group members wait six months before checking up on someone who has stopped coming, the probability of that person returning to active involvement is only 24 to 32 percent. When the follow up occurs within a couple of weeks, the probability of return to active involvement goes up to 89 to 94 percent. The more time that goes by without contact, the less likely it is that the person who has stopped coming will return.

If contact is made quickly, a phone call to indicate that the person was missed is often sufficient. The more time goes by, the more important that the contact be made in person. NEVER make people feel guilty for their absence. Simply let them know they were missed. If there is hesitancy for the next session, ask whether anything disturbing happened in the group. The feedback will help you make needed changes and may help you recover members who would otherwise be lost.

11. Be sure there is adequate communication between leaders of the new group and others in the church. The new group may often be the first "port of entry" for a young adult into the life of your church. The young adults shouldn't be put under pressure about further involvement, but it's important for the minister and others involved in member recruitment to know of that person's activity. A short visit at that person's home by the minister or another church leader can help reinforce the church's interest and may help bring that person a step closer to church membership.

12. Remember that young adults are searching for intimacy. The quality of what happens between people in the group is of greater importance to the group's success than any particular matter of content or style. Continually monitor the amount of caring and mutual support happening in the group. In one sense all church groups are "support groups" even if that is not the stated agenda.

Staffing for Young Adult Growth

Steve Clapp

Church staff members who are not themselves young adults can make significant contributions to the church's young adult ministry by the openness with which they relate to others and by the help they provide to other church leaders.

Most churches in the United States and Canada aren't large enough to have more than one minister on the church staff, and many churches share that person's time with another congregation. In most situations, that minister is older than the young adult age range. That minister's style and concern, however, are still important in developing successful young adult ministry.

When a church has more than one professional staff member—minister plus associate minister(s), director of Christian education, music director, business administrator, etc.—there is merit in trying to balance the age range represented by the staff. If the senior pastor is in his or her forties, fifties, or sixties, consider hiring a second staff person who is between twenty and forty. It is good for young adults to have a young adult with whom they can identify on the church staff. A young adult staff member can make a great difference in the life of the church.

Remember, however, that there is a danger in a group becoming too dependent on the leadership and personality of a particular staff member (or a particular volunteer, for that matter). It is very common for singles groups, in particular, to be formed around the personality of a young adult single on staff, and then to be in trouble as that person gets married or moves to another position. A broad leadership base needs to be established.

The Wesley Kolbe study of young adults and the church referred to in "Young Adults in the '90s" showed that young adults do base a large part of their opinion of a given church on the attitude of the minister and other staff. Thus how the church is staffed is an important considera-tion in overall young adult ministry.

- Staff members, regardless of age, responsibili-ties, or church size, need to understand, accept, and genuinely like young adults in all their diversity. They also need to understand the desire for intimacy that is especially strong in young adults.
- Staff members should have some under-standing of the ways in which young adult attitudes may differ from those of older adults in the church. The staff needs to help older church members learn to accept some of those differences.
- Staff members should work for the integra-tion of young adults in all phases of church leadership, not just in groups that are desig-nated as "young adult." See the chapter on "Young Adults in Church Leadership."
- Young adults in the church should have in-volvement in the selection of staff members. Try to have young adults on your personnel committee or pastor parish committee so that

they are a part of selecting the minister and other staff members and so that they can adequately represent young adult concerns to the staff.

• Staff members should seek young adult input and advice concerning the life of the church. There is a tendency for clergy especially (and sometimes other professional staff members) to be too dependent on the counsel of only a small group of church leaders, most of whom are often well out of the young adult years. Young adults are themselves always the best authority on young adult ministry and on building sensitivity to young adult needs in the church.

• Staff members need to see themselves as helping involve young adults in conducting the church's ministry rather than just focusing on ministry to young adults. Young adults certainly need to receive the church's ministry to others. Staff members can play a key role in setting those expectations.

• Staff members are the ones most likely to be introduced to visitors at worship services. In addition to whatever registration process is used by the church, staff members should take initiative to be sure that the names of new young adults are passed on to appropriate groups in the church so that the new people are included in invitations and activities.

RESOURCES

The resources shared in this final chapter will be helpful to you in better understanding young adults and in developing meaningful programs to reach them. This is a selective listing, including resources that are of high quality. Most are books, but a few videos, tapes, newsletters, and organizations have been included.

About Young Adults and Related Concerns

American Demographics. A monthly publication that contains continuing updates not only on young adults but on many facets of American life. This should be of primary interest to people in regional and national denominational positions, but some congregations may also find the information helpful and appreciate it in their libraries. For information, write: American Demographics, 108 N. Cayuga Street, Ithaca, NY 14850.

The Challenge of Single Adult Ministry, by Douglas Johnson. Judson Press. An overview on work with single adults.

Christian Education as Evangelism, by Steve Clapp. *faithQuest*. How to use Christian education classes and small groups in ways that further the growth of the church. Strategies for work with young adults and others. How to develop special ministries to people often overlooked.

Developing Faith in Young Adults, by Robert Gribbon. Alban Institute. On effective ministry with young adults. Gribbon discusses what young adults are looking for from the church and how the church can respond.

Faith-Sharing Video Kit, by Eddie Fox and George Morris. A video cassette, divided into six segments with print resources, offering practical help to church members wanting to share their faith positively with others. It is useful for work with adults of any age but is especially valuable for young adults. Developed for the United Methodist Church but applicable to any denomination. Order from Discipleship Resources (in the "Organizations" listing).

Forming Bible Study Groups, by Steve Clapp and Gerald Peterson. *faithQuest*. A practical guide to the formation of Bible study groups in the church.

Giving the Ministry Away, by Rick Hurst and Terry Hershey. Four tapes on leadership training for single and young adult ministry. Order from Christian Focus (in the "Organizations" listing).

Handbook on Congregational Ministries with Young Adults, edited by Myrna Burkholder. Developed by the Mennonite Board of Missions and specific to that denomination but included here because there are many ideas that will be helpful to any church. Order from the Mennonite Board (in the "Organizations" listing).

Ideas and Suggestions for District Young Adult Ministries, edited by Lorn Waggy. Written by young adults in the Church of the Brethren. The focus is on that denomination's ministry, but it gives an overview of strategies for use at the regional or ecumenical level. Order from the Church of the Brethren (in the "Organizations" listing).

Ministry with Black Single Adults, by Sharon Patterson. Discipleship Resources. About ministry to a frequently overlooked group.

The People's Religion, by George Gallup, Jr. and Jim Castelli. Macmillan. Brings together the most recent information from Gallup polls and related studies concerning religious beliefs and practices in the United States. There are many insights for work with young adults and for the broader outreach of the church. Any church leaders interested in understanding the overall shape of religious belief in America and the factors that draw people to or keep them away from the church will want to read this book.

Plain Talk about Church Growth, by Steve Clapp. *faithQuest*. Facing barriers to church growth, including the attitudes of people already in the church, and ways to overcome those barriers.

Singles Care for One Another, by Karen Greenwaldt. Discipleship Resources. Guidance for work with singles of any age but especially relevant for work with young adults.

Young Adult Ministry, by Terry Hershey. Group Books. An overall guide to young adult ministry, with a slightly greater emphasis on outreach to singles than to couples. Contains many helpful class/group program ideas as well as many suggested resources.

Young Adult Ministry, by Terry Hershey. A 72-minute video cassette divided into four training sessions for people working with young adult ministry. Order from Christian Focus (in the "Organizations" listing).

For Use by Young Adults and Young Adult Groups

The Caring Question, by Donald and Nancy Tubesing. Augsburg Publishing House. Especially for young families, this book helps deal with the concern of too many things to do and too little time. Sunday school discussion material to help young adults strike a healthy balance between caring for others and caring for themselves.

Clear-Headed Choices in a Sexually Confused World, by Terry Hershey. Group Books. Material for discussion about sexuality for those in their 20's and 30's.

Covenant Bible Study Series. Relational Bible study books published by *faithQuest*. Recommended for the kinds of young adult classes and groups discussed in this book. Each contains material for 10 sessions.

The Lord's Prayer, by Mary Sue Rosenberger.
Disciplines for Spiritual Growth,
            by Karen Peterson Miller.
Sermon on the Mount, by Robert C. Bowman
Psalms, by John David Bowman
Love and Justice, by Eva O'Diam
The Life of David, by Larry Fourman.
Presence and Power, by Robert W. Dell.

Creating Quality Relationships in a Fast-Paced World, by Denny Rydberg. Group Books. A 12-week course for a young adult study group aimed at helping people relate to God, friends, spouse, co-workers.

Creative Bible Studies for Young Adults, by Denny Rydberg. Group Books. Twenty Bible studies are included in this book for young adult groups. They touch on issues of stress, success, discipleship, and faith.

For Everything There Is A Season, by Karen Greenwaldt. Upper Room Books. An inspirational collection of meditations written by and for single adults.

Freedom of Simplicity, by Richard Foster. Harper & Row. A challenging look at contemporary lifestyles and the needs of the environment and the poor.

Getting Your Act Together, Four-part video series produced by Student/Young Adult Service, Mennonite Board of Missions. This discussion series features Tom Sine and Keith Miller for single young adults interested in reflecting on singleness and spiritual growth.

Go Away—Come Closer, by Terry Hershey. Word. Helps young adults (and people of any age) understand the tension between the desire for intimacy and the fear of intimacy.

Intimacy—The Longing of Every Human Heart, by Terry Hershey. Harvest House. Describes intimacy as a journey. For study by young adult singles and couples.

Lifestyle Small Group Series, by Peter Marconi, Richard Peace, and Lyman Coleman. Serendipity House. Bible studies for young adults, with seven lessons in each booklet. Career: Take This Job and Love It; Stressed Out: Keeping It Together When It's Falling Apart; Singles: Looking Out For Number One; Success: Does the One With the Most Toys Win?

Man's Search for Meaning, by Victor Frankl. Pocket Books. Frankl writes about his experiences in a Nazi camp and about the insights he gained into the meaning of life and the importance of relationships with others. In the Wesley Kolbe study, this book was named by several young adults as one of the most influential they had read.

Parent Education—A Guide for Family Enrichment Classes, by Rosemary Tweet and Ted Schwarz. Discipleship Resources. A resource to set up groups for young adults who are parents or soon to become parents.

The Passionate Life, by Sam Keen. Harper & Row. Study for those seriously wanting to discover how to have an enjoyable, meaningful life. Will provoke some stimulating discussions.

Remember Lot's Wife, by April Yamasaki. *faithQuest*. A book of devotional readings on unnamed women in the Bible. Young adults will be especially responsive to this book.

The Road Less Traveled, by Scott Peck. Touchstone. Psychiatrist Peck challenges the reader to come to greater self-understanding. In the Wesley Kolbe survey, this was one of the books several young adults cited as one of the most influential they had read.

The Success Fantasy, by Anthony Campolo. Victor. A good, practical book for groups wanting to explore what real success means and for people struggling with low self-esteem because they have not achieved success by the standards of society.

When All You've Ever Wanted Isn't Enough, by Harold Kusher. Summit. Helps people deal with what is truly important in life and questions many of the assumptions on which so many of us make decisions.

Organizational and Denominational Information

The following addresses of denominational offices and selected organizations may be helpful to you in obtaining assistance in the development of young adult ministries. Many denominations have relevant publications specific to their structure and theology and may also have staff members with particular expertise in young adult ministry.

Alban Institute, 4124 Nebraska Ave., N.W., Washington, DC 20016. Publishers of the newsletter *Action Information* and of various studies about young adults.

American Baptist Churches in the U.S.A., Box 851, Valley Forge, PA 19482.

Assemblies of God, 1445 Boonville Ave., Springfield, MO 56802.

Christian Church (Disciples of Christ), Division of Homeland Ministries, Box 1986, Indianapolis, IN 46206.

Christian Focus, P.O. Box 2658, Woodinville, WA 98072. Terry Hershey's organization. He provides many helpful materials for young adult ministry.

Church of the Brethren General Board, 1451 Dundee Ave., Elgin, IL 60120.

Church of God, 1303 E. 5th St., Anderson, IN 46018.

Church of the Nazarene, 6401 The Paseo, Kansas City, MO 64131.

Discipleship Resources, Box 840, Nashville, TN 37202. Resources from the United Methodist Church including many appropriate for ecumenical use.

Episcopal Church, U.S.A., Episcopal Church Center, 815 2nd Ave., New York, NY 10017.

Evangelical Lutheran Church in America, 8765 W. Higgins Rd., Chicago, IL 60631.

faithQuest., 451 Dundee Ave., Elgin, IL 60120. The ecumenical research and publishing division of Brethren Press.

Friends United Meeting, 101 Quaker Hill Dr., Richmond, IN 47374.

Group Publishing, P.O. Box 481, Loveland, CO 80539. Primarily a publisher of youth work materials but also some young adult resources.

Lutheran Church - Missouri Synod, 1333 S. Kirkwood Rd., St. Louis, MO 63122.

Mennonite Board of Missions, Box 1245, Elkhart, IN 46515.

Paulist Press, 997 Macarthur Blvd., Mahwah, NJ 07430. A prominent Catholic publisher with many books and materials for young adult groups.

Presbyterian Church in America, 1852 Century Pl., Atlanta, GA 30345.

Presbyterian Church (U.S.A.), 100 Witherspoon St., Louisville, KY 40202.

Princeton Religious Research Center, Box 310, 53 Bank St., Princeton, NJ 08542. Research on religious beliefs and church activity in the United States. Reports, newsletters, updates.

Small Group Letter, P.O. Box 1164, Dover, NJ 07801. Helpful newsletter for those doing small group work.

Southern Baptist Convention, 127 9th Ave. N., Nashville, TN 37234.

United Church of Christ, Board for Homeland Ministries, 700 Prospect Ave., Cleveland, OH, 44115.

United Methodist Church, 1908 Grand Ave., Nashville, TN 37202.

United Pentecostal Church, 8855 Dunn Rd., Hazelwood, MO 63042.

U.S. Catholic Conference, 8900 Harewood Rd., N.E., Washington, DC 20017.